OCCULT SECRETS OF VRIL

Robert Sepehr

Printed in the United States of America

First Printing, 2015

ISBN 978-1-943494-02-6

Atlantean Gardens
5334 Lindley Ave #133
Encino, CA 91316

www.AtlanteanGardens.org

Table of Contents

Introduction

Is mankind on the threshold of a new age of enlightenment? Or are we descending a dwindling spiral, doomed to repeat the lessons from history which we either forget or never seem to learn?

In pre-WWII Germany, the Vril Society used the swastika (卍) emblem to link Eastern and Western occultism. They advanced the idea of a subterranean matriarchal utopia ruled by a race of Aryan beings who had mastered a mysterious force called Vril. This breakaway civilization had survived the antediluvian cataclysms which ended the ice age, and passed on their guarded occult knowledge through initiation into sacred mystery schools. Vril was known to these mystics as a natural and abundant energy, having disseminated it's divine wisdom world wide under many names. The Chinese referred to it as "chi", the Hindu as "prana", and the Japanese as "reiki". Albert Pike said: "There is in nature one most potent force, by means whereof a single man, who could possess himself of it, and should know how to direct it, could revolutionize and change the face of the world." Helena Blavatski, the foundress of the Theosophical Society, described this Vril energy as an aether stream that could be transformed into a physical force. What are the *Occult Secrets of Vril?*

Chapter 1

A growing number of independent researchers believe that the world's fascination with nuclear war is just the latest episode in a series of tragedies that humanity seems intent on repeating.

Hindu tales speak of swift flying craft called vimanas. Vimanas were flying palaces or chariots, and were said to have the ability to deliver explosives at very high altitude and speed.(2) Sir Monier Monier-Williams (1819 – 1899) was the second Boden Professor of Sanskrit at Oxford University, England. He defines Vimana as "a car or a chariot of the gods, any mythical self-moving aerial car (sometimes serving as a seat or throne, sometimes self-moving and carrying its occupant through the air; other descriptions make the Vimana more like a house or palace, and one kind is said to be seven stories high)", and quotes the Pushpaka Vimana of Ravana as an example.

In some modern Indian languages like Hindi, vimana means "aircraft", for example in the town name Vimanapura (a suburb of Bangalore). In the Mahabharata, the Asura Maya had a Vimana with four strong wheels, which measured twelve cubits in circumference. The Ramayana describes the pushpaka ("flowery") vimana of Ravana as follows:

Depiction of a prehistoric flying machine called Vimana

FIGURE 1

"The Pushpaka Vimana that resembles the Sun and belongs to my brother was brought by the powerful Ravana; that aerial and excellent Vimana going everywhere at will. That chariot resembling a bright cloud in the sky. And the King [Rama] got in, and the excellent chariot at the command of the Raghira, rose up into the higher atmosphere."

⬦⬦⬦

Ancient Indo-Aryan texts describe great, epic wars, and they have made a tremendous impression on generations. These armies used weapons that, as bizarre as it sounds, could literally level the land like a moving force field.(3) Ancient Indian texts contain classifications of words that stretch the imagination for certain measurements of length; there is one word for the distance of light-years and another for the length of an atom. It has been argued that only a society that possessed direct knowledge of nuclear energy would have the need for such nomenclature. (2, 3)

Robert Oppenheimer (1904 - 1967) was a Jewish American theoretical physicist, best known as the scientific director of the Manhattan Project,

Robert Oppenheimer and Albert Einstein.

FIGURE 2

Atomic bomb

FIGURE 3

the effort to develop,during World War II, the first nuclear weapons. He is often remembered as the "father of the atomic bomb", having worked closely with Albert Einstein.

After witnessing the first nuclear explosion, at the Trinity test site, on July 16, 1945, Oppenheimer remarked that it brought to his mind words from Chapter 11, Verse 32 of the Bhagavad Gita: Now I am become Death, the destroyer of worlds.(2)

Some researchers claim the vast empty deserts on a number of continents today are the possible result of (pre-historic) nuclear warfare. In fact, Aryan sacred writings are full of descriptions which sound like atomic explosions and fallout, as experienced by helpless victims in Hiroshima and Nagasaki.(6, 10)

When asked during an interview by a student: How do you feel after having exploded the first atomic bomb? Robert Oppenheimer replied simply and directly: "Not first atomic bomb, first atomic bomb in modern times."(9)

Professor Oppenheimer strongly held the conviction that radioactive weapons were detonated in ancient warfare, as recorded in the old scriptures. What made him believe that these were nuclear battles were the eerily accurate descriptions of the weapons, and their effects, as used in the wars described in the epic Vedic literature. These descriptions match closely with witness testimonial descriptions of modern nuclear detonations. A description of the total destructive power of these weapons appears in the Ramayana, which reads: It was a weapon so powerful that it could destroy the earth in an instant. A great soaring sound in smoke and flames and on it sits death.(5) The Ramayana, attributed to the poet Valmiki, was written during

Temple relief at the Ellora Caves, India

FIGURE 4

7

the first century A.D., although it is based on oral traditions that go back six or seven centuries earlier.

Further examples of possible atomic battles in ancient times appear in the Drona Parva, a section of the Mahabharata. The passage tells of fierce combat where explosions of 'final weapons' decimate entire armies, causing crowds of warriors with steeds, elephants, and weapons to be carried away as if they were the dry leaves of trees.(9) The Mahabharata, attributed to the sage Vyasa, was written down from 540 to 300 B.C., and tells the legends of the Bharatas, a Vedic Aryan group. It has been suggested that Oppenheimer was referring to the Brahmastra weapon mentioned in these Vedic texts. Consider these verses from the ancient Mahabharata:

ᐧᐧᐧ

- Gurkha, flying a swift and powerful vimana [fast aircraft], hurled a single projectile charged with all the power of the Universe. An incandescent column of smoke and flame as bright as the thousand suns arose in all its splendor, a perpendicular explosion with its billowing smoke clouds, the cloud of smoke rising after its first explosion formed into expanding round circles like the opening of giant parasols.

- It was an unknown weapon, an iron thunderbolt, a gigantic messenger of death, which reduced to ashes the entire race of the Vrishnis and the Andhakas. The corpses were so burned as to be unrecognizable. The hair and nails fell out; Pottery broke without apparent cause, And the birds turned white. After a few hours All foodstuffs were infected, to escape from this fire, the soldiers threw themselves in streams to wash themselves and their equipment.

- Dense arrows of flame, like a great shower, issued forth, encompassing the enemy. A thick gloom swiftly settled upon the hosts. All points of the compass were lost in darkness. Fierce wind began to blow upward, showering dust and gravel. Birds croaked madly the very elements seemed disturbed.

- The earth shook, scorched by the terrible violent heat of this weapon. Elephants burst into flame and ran to and fro in a frenzy over a vast area, other animals crumpled to the ground and died. From all points of the compass the arrows of flame rained continuously and fiercely. (2,9)

Although Oppenheimer never formally converted to any other religion, and never referred to himself as a Hindu, the ancient Aryan Vedic philosophy did influence him greatly. He never openly prayed to any deities, nor went to a Mandir (Hindu temple). He was never a follower in a devotional sense, but he did take lessons in Sanskrit so he could better understand the Bhagavad Gita in its native tongue. His brother said that Oppenheimer found the Bhagavad Gita: Very easy and quite marvelous, and was really taken by the charm and the general wisdom of the Bhagavad Gita. Robert Oppenheimer was also famously quoted as saying that: Access to the Vedas is the greatest privilege this century may claim over all previous centuries.(1)

Glass Scarab in King Tut's Pendant

FIGURE 5

In 1996, Vincenzo de Michele, an Italian mineralogist spotted an unusual yellow-green gem in the middle of one of Tutankhamun's necklaces. The beautiful scarab at the center of King Tut's pendant was tested and found to be glass, but it turned out to be much older than the earliest Egyptian civilization. The fission track dates of the glass indicate that it is at least 28 million years old. (20)

Geologists traced its origins to unexplained chunks of glass, called Libyan Desert Glass, found scattered in the sand in a remote region of the Sahara Desert. The glass itself, however, is a scientific enigma. How did it get to be there and who or what made it?

Libyan desert glass

FIGURE 6

Libyan Desert Glass (LDG) is a natural glass made of silica (silicon dioxide), and easily found. It is dispersed along the Libyan Desert: scattered throughout the western desert of West Egypt, by the Libyan-Egyptian border. The glass is a form of tektite, a word which comes from the Greek word "tektos", meaning molten. Scientists say the glass in this region is the largest known deposit of a natural silica glass on the planet Earth (about 98% SiO2). The transparent, and sometimes translucent, pieces are clear-to-opaque white or yellow-to-green in color, and they glitter like gems in the bright desert sun. They vary in size from small pieces to large chunks weighing over 20 pounds. The glass was known to the ancient Egyptians, who called it "The Rock of God"; while it was even known to prehistoric people as it was used for palaeolithic tools, such as sharp blades, dating to about 10,000 years ago.

An Austrian astrochemist, Christian Koeberl, established that the desert glass had been formed at a temperature so hot that there could be only one known cause to account for the tremendous heat: a meteorite impacting with Earth. Yet there were no visible signs of a suitable impact crater where this glass is located, even in satellite images. (12)

Another explanation is that the heat that formed the desert glass had a terrestrial source, one that included atomic war, using weapons capable of melting sand. In his book, *The Wars of Gods and Men*, Zecharia Sitchin puts forward this alternative high-tech explanation for the sudden extreme heat.(6) Sitchin, a strong proponent for advanced ancient civilizations with sophisticated technology, describes what the Greeks wrote down concerning the battle between Zeus and the the Titans:

◇◇

"The hot vapor lapped around the Titans, of Gaea born, flame unspeakable rose bright to the upper air. The Flashing glare of the Thunder-Stone, its lightning, blinded their eyes-so strong it was. Astounding heat seized Chaos. It seemed as if Earth and wide Heaven above had come together, a mighty crash, as though Earth was hurled to ruin. Also the winds brought rumbling, earthquake and dust storm, thunder and lightning."(6)

◇◇

He argues that the abrupt end to some ancient civilizations in our mythologies may have been based on real events: cataclysms due to the prehistoric use of nuclear weaponry. In this verse, Zeus is conquering Typhon:

✧✧

"A flame shot forth from the stricken lord in the dim, rugged, secluded valley of the Mount, when he was smitten. A great part of
huge earth was scorched by the terrible vapor, melting as tin melts
when heated by man's art, in the glow of a blazing fire did the earth
melt down."(3)

✧✧

During the first Egyptian Pyramid War waged between Horus and
Seth, the moment Horus strikes, "He let loose against them a storm which
they could neither see with their eyes, nor hear with their ears. It brought
death to all of them in a single moment."(3)

The Bible also contains incidents which many researchers attribute to
ancient nuclear warfare, such as the destruction of Sodom and Gomorrah
(Gen 18:27): (Abraham) looked toward Sodom and Gomorrah, and he saw
a smoke rising from the earth, as smoke of a furnace.(4)

Beginning in 1999, archaeologists specializing in the Near East saw
mounting empirical evidence that the demise of Sumer (and Akkad,
Sumer's northern extension) coincided with an abrupt climate change.
An initial study by Harvey Weiss and Timothy C. Wieskel of Harvard
University placed the date at about 4000 years ago. A subsequent study,
published in the April 2000 edition of Geology by H.M. Cullen (et al.),
reinforced this finding. Based on studies of unexplained aridity and
wind-blown dust storms and radiocarbon dating, they reported that their
readings indicated a date of about 4000 years ago, with about a 100 year
margin of error.(7)

A major study published in the April 2001 issue of Journal Science,
authored by Peter B. deMenocal of Columbia University, paid particular
attention to sedimentary remains of Tephra (fragmental material usually
attributed to a volcanic eruption), and concluded that the rock fragments
confirmed the date of around 2000 BC, also about 4000 years ago.(8) According to Zecharia Sitchin:

"The only explanation for these broken and blackened stones in the Sinai and the windblown desolation in Mesopotamia can be the tale of the Erra Epos, (reflected in the biblical tale of Sodom and Gomorrah): not an eruption by a non-existent volcano, but the use of nuclear weapons in 2024 B.C."(3)

The first detonation of an atomic bomb by the United States in New Mexico at the Trinity test site in 1945 created so much heat that it formed a crater of radioactive glass in the desert about 10 feet deep and over 1,000 feet in width. This is the same type of glass that is found in India, Egypt, and many other locations.

Crater made by test of first atomic bomb, Trinity in 1945

FIGURE 7

Many in the scientific community believe that the desert glass resulted from a meteorite impact; however, no crater has ever been found. The tremendous heat, pressure, and shock waves from massive meteorite impacts alter the materials near or directly beneath a meteor impact site, and as a result they are known as "impactites". Sand melts into impact glasses, and rocks get shattered and compressed into breccias (broken fragments of rock cemented together). Melted glasses and fragments of sediments become embedded in the fine grained matrix, the cement of the breccias. Yet, much of the desert glass is clear of the embedded sediments one would expect to find, if it were from a meteor impact.

Libyan Desert Glass (LDG) is made of silica (silicon dioxide)

FIGURE 8

Some scientists propose that a meteor exploded above the ground, leaving no impact crater, yet producing enough heat to melt and glassify the surface material below. This scenario is similar to an air burst event, like the one which is often described in association with the 1908 Tunguska explosion over Siberia.

Tunguska event of 1908

FIGURE 17

The Tunguska explosion knocked down an estimated 80 million trees over an area of over 2,000 square kilometers (830 sq mi), and, if the measurement could have been taken, the shock wave from the blast would have measured 5.0 on the Richter scale. An explosion of this magnitude would be capable of destroying an entire metropolitan city, but due to the remoteness of the Siberian location, there were no documented fatalities.(22)

However, there are those who say the glass couldn't have been fused from the local exposed sandstone because both the sand and the dunes are not older than one million years while the Libyan Desert Glass is reported to be over 28 million years old.(21) I think it is fair to say this topic is not yet closed and deserves more serious investigation and debate.

Chapter 2

American attorney, Confederate officer, writer, and Freemason, Albert Pike said:

◇◇◇

"There is in nature one most potent force, by means whereof a single man, who could possess himself of it, and should know how to direct it, could revolutionize and change the face of the world." (13)

◇◇◇

In India, such potent energy is equated with prana. Prana is the Sanskrit word for "life force". In Jainism it also means vital principle, and in Indian medicine, yoga, and martial arts, the term refers to a cosmic energy that permeates all matter. The universal principle of energy, or force, responsible for the body's life, heat and maintenance, prana is the sum total of all energy that is manifest in the universe. While prana is the general name of the life force, the prana vayu is one of its specific functions.

In Ayurveda, tantra and Tibetan medicine "prana vayu" is the basic vayu from which all the other vayus arise. The word vayu translates literally as "wind" or "air", connoting all-pervading movement. The root 'va' means "that which flows". A vayu is a vehicle for activities and experiences within the body, or a "force" that moves throughout the system controlling functions such as breathing, digestion, and nerve impulses. In the human body, this universal prana has been said by ancient alchemists to move in specific ways in specific regions in the body, regulating and controlling physical and mental function. Prana is analogous to qi or chi in China.

In traditional Chinese culture, chi (also qi or ki) is an active principle forming part of any living thing. Chi is frequently translated as "natural energy", "life force", or "energy flow". Chi is the central underlying principle in traditional Chinese medicine, Taoist philosophy and martial arts. The literal translation of chi is "breath" or "air". Some believe chi is a separate force from the physical world, while others think chi comes from physical matter.(53) Still others, especially Chinese Buddhists and Taoists, hold that matter arises from chi.(48) The quality, quantity and balance of Ch'i is believed to be essential to maintaining health and achieving a long life. Livia Kohn, author of *Health and Long Life: The Chinese Way*, explains it this way:

Qi (chi) is the basic material of all that exists. It animates life and furnishes functional power of events. Qi (chi) is the root of the human body; its quality and movement determine human health. There is a normal or healthy amount of qi (chi) in every person, and health manifests in its balance and harmony, its moderation and smoothness of flow. (48)

Breath control is considered especially fundamental to balancing the levels of ch'i in one's body. Controlled and meditative breathing, called hsing-ch'i, allows ch'i to permeate the entire body by imagining the breath as a visible universal force or current moving through the body.(48)

In Japan, this universal force is called reiki, and is usually discussed in the context of stress reduction, relaxation and healing. It is administered by "laying on hands" and is based on the idea that an unseen life force energy flows through all beings and is what causes us to be alive. The word reiki is made of two Japanese words - "rei" which means "God's Wisdom or the Higher Power" and "ki" which is "life force energy". So reiki is actually "spiritually guided life force energy."(53)

Vril is another name of this life force energy that theoretically fills the universe and all living beings. Helena Blavatski, the foundress of the Theosophical Society, described this Vril energy as an aether stream that could be transformed into a physical force. The Vril Society was a secret organization in Germany devoted to mastering and this unseen force of nature. They accumulated and combined the guarded alchemical knowledge of this life force contained in Sufism, Aryan Hindu mysticism, Theosophy, Nordic and Sumerian mythology, Pagan sex magick, channeled material and the Kabbalah. According to esoteric and yoga teachings, sexual energies can be channeled upward to develop our energy centers or chakra system and higher energy bodies. Tantra and kundalini yoga were two ancient Aryan techniques utilized by the Vril Society to harness this sexual energy: Tantra in ritualized male-female interaction and kundalini yoga in strict individual practice; both methods entail semen retention. In the book, *Morning of the Magicians*, authors Jacques Bergier and Louis Pauwels say:

> This secret society was founded, literally, on Bulwer Lytton's novel The Coming Race (1871). The book describes a race of men psychically far in advance of our own. They have acquired powers over themselves and over things that made them almost godlike. For the moment they are in hiding. They are said to live in caves in the center of the Earth. Soon they will emerge to reign over us. (14)

The Vril Society expanded on an ancient archetype that already held the attention of alchemists and magicians, which was merely re-interpret-

Edward Bulwer-Lytton (1803 – 1873)

FIGURE 9

ed, by Edward Bulwer-Lytton, in light of that age of occult revival and scientific progress. Lytton, himself, was an initiate of the Rosicrucian order. (15) In his book, *Vril: The Coming Race*, the people of the subterranean civilization use their understanding of nature, eco-friendly energy and Vril technology to operate and govern the world.(16) They, having mastered many physical laws, such as gravity, were able to fly on vril-powered anti-gravity disc craft. The vegetarian Vril race are, by their own reckoning, racially and culturally superior to everyone else on Earth, both above and below the surface crust. Lytton's book explains that the race of Vril people are:

◇◇◇

Descended from the same ancestors as the great Aryan family, from which in varied streams has flowed the dominant civilization of the world.(16)

◇◇◇

Author J. Bergier says of Vril, and of Lytton: "Through his romantic works of fiction he expressed the conviction that there are beings endowed with superhuman powers. These beings will supplant us and bring about a formidable mutation in the elect of the human race."

After fleeing Germany in 1933, Dr. Willy Ley, one of the world's greatest rocket experts, said:

◇◇◇

"The Vril Society, which formed shortly before the Nazis came to power, believed they had secret knowledge that would enable them to change their race and become equals of the men hidden in the bowels of the Earth. Methods of concentration, a whole system of internal gymnastics by which they would be transformed. These methods of concentration were probably based on Ignatius Loyola's Spiritual Exercises. The Jesuit techniques of concentration and visualization are similar to many occult teachings, especially in shamanic cults and Tibetan Buddhism. The Nazi's revered these Jesuit Spiritual Exercises, which they believed had been handed down from ancient Masters of Atlantis. The occultists of the time knew that Ignatius was a Basque (some claimed that the Basque people were the last remnant of the Atlantean race) and the proper use of these techniques would enable the reactivation of the Vril for the dominance of the Teutonic race over all others. The Vril Society believed that whoever becomes master of the Vril will be the master of himself, of others around him and of the world. The belief was that the world will change and the "Lords" will emerge from the center of the Earth. Unless we have made an alliance with them and become "Lords" ourselves, we shall find ourselves among the slaves, on the dung-heap that will nourish the roots of the New Cities that will arise."(17)

John Martin (1789–1854): Pandemonium. Louvre Museum

FIGURE 10

This was the psychic force, or universal free energy, behind the paranormal technology that the Nazis and their inner occult circle were so desperately trying to harness. In the book, *The Unknown Hitler*, Wulf Schwarzwaller says:

In Berlin, Haushofer had founded the Luminous Lodge or the Vril Society. The Lodge's objective was to explore the origins of the Aryan race and to perform exercises in concentration to awaken the forces of "Vril". Haushofer was a student of the Russian magician and metaphysician George Gurdjieff. Both Gurdjieff and Haushofer maintained that they had contacts with secret Tibetan lodges that possessed the secret of the "Superman." The Lodge included Hitler, Aalfred, Rosenberg, Himmler, Goring and Hitler's subsequent personal physician Dr. Morell. It is also known that Aleister Crowley and Gurdjieff sought contact with Hitler. Hitler's unusual powers of suggestion become more understandable if one keeps in mind that he had access to the "secret" psychological techniques of Gurdjieff which, in turn, were based on the teachings of the Sufis and the Tibetan lamas and familiarized him with the Zen teaching of the Japanese Society of the Green Dragon. (18)

In Brad Steiger's book, *The Rainbow Conspiracy*, he summarizes a presentation given by the missing conspiracy researcher, Vladmir Terzinski, in the mid 1990's:

In his controversial presentation UFO Secrets of the Third Reich, Vladimir Terziski draws a connection between alien beings and such German secret societies as the Tempelhoff,the Thule, the Vril, and the Black Sun. Terziski tells of an "alien tutor race" that secretly began cooperating with certain German scientists in the late 1920's in underground bases and began to introduce their concepts of philosophical, cultural, and technological progress. With help from extraterrestrial intelligences, Terziski postulates, the Nazis mastered antigravity space flight, established space stations, accomplished time travel,and developed their spacecraft to warp speeds. At the same time the aliens "spread their Mephistophelean ideas" into the wider German population through the Thule and Vril Societies. Terziski maintains that antigravity research began in Germany in the 1920's with the first hybrid antigravity circular craft, the RFZ-1, constructed by the Vril Society. In 1942-43 a series of antigravity machines culminated in the giant 350-foot long, cigar-shaped Andromeda space station, which was constructed in old zeppelin hangars near Berlin by E4, the research and development arm of the SS. (19)

◇◇

The Allies confiscated every Nazi document they could find, and most documents are still classified 70 years after the war ended. It is well known that the Nazi elite had some highly classified technology, which was way ahead of their time. If technologically advanced subterranean civilizations do exist, and the Nazis did establish contact with this advanced race, then we could assume that this anti-gravity propulsion, rumored to have been developed by the Nazis, worked on the free energy principles of Vril.

Alleged photograph of German disc craft in 1945

FIGURE 11

After World War II, and the occupation of Germany that followed, Allied military commanders were stunned to discover the penetrating depth of the Nazi's closest guarded state secrets. The world's best intelligence organization was not the least of these revelations. Also discovered were massive and meticulous research file on secret societies, metaphysics, genetics, alternative energy, and other scientific pursuits that boggled the imagination of the Allied command. Even more spectacular was an entire web of underground rocket and alternative propulsion factories with an accompanying free-energy technology that still defies conventional belief.

FIGURE 12

Missing U-boat fleets possessing the most advanced submarine technology in the world left many wondering if the Nazis had escaped with yet more secrets or even with Hitler himself.

The SS E-IV was a unit of the Order of the Black Sun, an occult Nazi organization, which was tasked with researching alternative energies to make the Third Reich independent of scarce fuel oil for war production.

German U-Boat

FIGURE 21

Their work included developing alternative energies, fuel sources and motors, including EMG (Electro-Magnetic-Gravitic) engines.

By 1939, this group developed a revolutionary engine which created powerful rotating electromagnetic fields that affected gravity and reduced mass. It was designated the Thule Triebwerk (Thrustwork, a.ka. Tachyonator-7 drive) and was to be installed into Vril disc craft called Haunebu (I-IV).

Nazi occult research also extended into the investigation of paranormal and metaphysical phenomenon. They were interested in unlocking the full human potential, which included psychic abilities and the detection and manipulation of etheric energies. Much of this research has been kept from the public after WW2 and transferred into black ops projects run by organizations such as the CIA. There were some scientists, however, that managed to study and publish their findings independently.

Dr. Wilhelm Reich (1897-1957) was an Austrian-born psychoanalyst noted historically for his work in psychiatry. He said he wanted to "attack the neurosis by its prevention rather than treatment." However, Dr. Reich's greatest scientific contributions involved his work in biophysics, which has been almost totally erased from history.

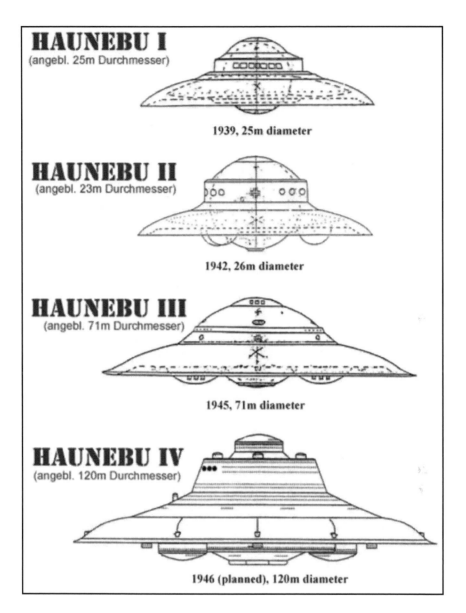

HAUNEBU I
(angebl. 25m Durchmesser)

1939, 25m diameter

HAUNEBU II
(angebl. 23m Durchmesser)

1942, 26m diameter

HAUNEBU III
(angebl. 71m Durchmesser)

1945, 71m diameter

HAUNEBU IV
(angebl. 120m Durchmesser)

1946 (planned), 120m diameter

FIGURE 18

From the 1930s, he became an increasingly controversial figure; from 1932 until his death all his work was self-published. The controversy began when Dr. Reich began noticing an energetic connection that all living beings held in common. He called this mysterious force "orgone energy" or "orgone radiation", derived from "orgasm" and "organism", and the study of it "orgonomy."

Dr. Wilhelm Reich

FIGURE 52

Dr. Reich worked tirelessly for the next 40 years demonstrating its laws and studying its various manifestations. He published a series of papers on the idea of "orgastic potency," the ability to release the emotions from the muscles and lose the self in an uninhibited orgasm. He argued that psychic health and the ability to love depended on orgastic potency. He attempted to ground his orgasm theory in biology, exploring whether the libido in fact represented electricity or a chemical substance. Though one cannot see or smell it, his sensitive equipment could measure it. Dr. Reich bought an oscillograph and attached it to friends and students, who volunteered to arouse each other, while Reich read the tracings. He first said he had discovered a life force or cosmic energy, an extension of Freud's idea of the libido, in New York in 1939. After Reich had demonstrated the properties of orgone energy to Albert Einstein, the famous physicist exclaimed that, "this would be a bombshell to physics."

In 1933, Dr. Reich detailed a biological basis for neurosis in his book, *Character Analysis,* and provided an outline of his research which would lead him to the discovery of this vril-like cosmic energy. Experiments involving microorganisms and airborne infection opened the door to his experiments concerning radiation particles that he later called orgone.

Further experiments showed that this ever-present orgone energy would be repelled by metal objects and absorbed by organic material. He created devices to amplify and harness this energy which were composed of alternate layers of organic (wool) material and metal. Reich found that he could accumulate, concentrated, and utilize this field of orgone for health benefits of biological organisms. He called these elevator-sized box-shaped devices "orgone accumulators" and word got out about the dramatic and positive results he had been getting with human test subjects. Dr. Reich was able to watch orgone in the various forms it would take on within an accumulator, measuring orgone with a thermometer and an electroscope as well as with a Geiger counter. The forms manifested as a bluish-gray, fog-like formation; deeply blue-violet luminous dots or; whitish, rapid rays.

What Dr. Reich discovered astounded him, and was what appeared to be the vril energy responsible for the biological, orgiastic pulsation of life on Earth (and possibly the universe). During the course of his varied orgone experiments, he touched upon many aspects of science, including the disciplines of medicine, physics, cosmology and meteorology. He discovered atmospheric orgone and noticed that, in the presence of pollutants of various kinds, including electromagnetic emissions, the energy would become stagnant and cause illness and environmental damage. To counter the negative effects, Dr. Reich added long pipes to an orgone accumulator device and pointed it skyward to help balance the atmospheric orgone and bring rain. He called this device a "cloud buster."

In one experiment starting in October, 1954, Dr. Reich was successful in bringing rain to the desert around Tucson, Arizona. Even before the rain fell the newly-balanced orgone had caused the grass to grow and thrive in the desert. Rather than embracing Dr. Reich's discoveries, the politically-motivated scientific authorities responded with levels of anger and derision that bordered on hatred.

In the years to follow, the American government made an attempt to wipe the very word "orgone" from the English vocabulary, by banning the accumulator and destroying Dr. Reich's books and journals (burned by order of the court). After a lengthy harassment campaign by the FDA over the medical use of orgone that began in the mid 40s, Dr. Reich was sentenced to two years in prison, where he died serving time for no crimes committed in 1957.

Chapter 3

Behind all of these mysteries was an even deeper element: a secret order known to initiates as the Order of the Black Sun. This organization was so feared that it is now illegal to even print their symbols and insignia in modern Germany. It's roots stem from The Vril Society that began around the same time as the Thule Society, when Karl Haushofer founded the "Bruder des Lichts", which means Brothers of the Light, sometimes referred to as the Luminous Lodge. Whereas the Thule Society ended up focusing primarily upon materialistic and political agendas, the Vril Society put its attention on more metaphysical matters. This group was eventually renamed the Vril-Gesellschaft as it rose in prominence and united three major societies:

- **The Lords of the Black Stone (Teutonic Order)**
- **The Black Knights of the Thule Society**
- **The Black Sun, the elite branch of the SS**

When the German secret societies came into being after World War I, the world's leading authorities on archeology and linguistics, especially regarding ancient Sumer and Babylon, were primarily German. A medium named Maria Orsic began getting messages in an unknown language and couldn't transcribe them, so began meeting with key members of these societies, along with other mediums.

Maria Orsic

FIGURE 13

The messages supposedly came from the star system of Aldebaran, an orange giant located about 65 light years away in the zodiac constellation of Taurus, which they believed has two planets and were said to exist two classes of people - the Aryan or original "pure" race, and a subservient race which had devolved, or developed in a negative fashion, as a result of mutation from climatic changes likely due to nuclear fallout. From Peter Moon's book, *The Black Sun:*

A half billion years ago, the Aryans (Elohim or Elder Race) began to colonize our solar system as Aldebaran's became uninhabitable. Marduk, existing in what is today the asteroid belt , was the first to be colonized, then Mars. When they came to Earth, these Aryans were known as the Sumerians.

Robert Sepehr, Pergamon Museum, Berlin, Germany.

FIGURE 19

Compiled by Jan van Helsing, a more detailed summary of the messages the Vril medium had received over the years and which formed the basis for all further actions by the Vril-Gesellschaft. This material is not science fiction, but represents truly what was going on in the inner core of occult lodges such as Thule and Vril. It should be emphasized to the reader that even if you don't believe a word of this, that is not the point. They believed it and built at least two very complicated secret societies around it, and they became quite powerful and influential. Jan van Helsing relays:

The solar system Aldebaran has a sun around which revolve two inhabited planets. The population of the Aldebaran system is divided into the original "pure" race of people (Aryans) and several other human races that had devolved by genetic mutation from the parent population because of climatic changes brought about by nuclear war upon the planets. The more the races intermixed, the lower the spiritual development of these people collectively sank, which led to the situation that when the sun Aldebaran began expanding they could no longer maintain the space travel technology of their forefathers and could not leave the planets by their own means. The genetically degraded races, totally dependent upon the master race, had to be evacuated and were brought to other inhabitable planets. They colonized our solar system, starting with the planet Mallona (also called Maldek, Marduk or Phaeton among Russians) that existed at that time between Mars and Jupiter, now occupied by the asteroid belt. Mars was next. Despite their physical and cultural differences, all the races respected one another and did not interfere with each other, neither the so-called genetically "pure" people nor the mutated hybrid races. Each respected that the others just made their own developments [in contrast to what happens on Earth].

Members of the Vril Society believed that these ancient astronauts landed on Earth following global cataclysms and upheavals, when the planet became slowly habitable again. Re-establishing agricultural civilization in with rivers for irrigation, such as Mesopotamia, they formed the dominant ruling nobility of the Sumerians and various other early societies, governing through an elite bloodline and segregated caste system; interracial inter-breeding (mixing blood) was strictly taboo.

Robert Sepehr, Pergamon Museum, Berlin, Germany.

FIGURE 14

Hiroshi Oshima, the former Japanese Ambassador to Germany, believed that the noble castes in Japan, the Daimyo and the Samurai, were also descended from gods of celestial origin, which was similar to the Nazi theory that "the Nordic race did not evolve, but came directly down from heaven to settle on the Atlantic continent.

Hanuman's tale, as told in the epic Ramayana, is about the Hindu monkey god, one of the most celebrated and worshiped figures in Indian religion. He is also mentioned in several other texts, including Mahabharata, the various Puranas and some Jain texts. According to the Vedas, a god-like race calling themselves Aryans, known historically as 'serpent worshippers' (phallus and fertility cult), or the 'serpent seed', were agriculturalists that practiced animal husbandry. They eventually began to cross-breed Humans with apes or monkeys, producing a hybrid servant or worker. This ancient stone temple frieze depicts the "monkey army", their slave corps, building a bridge of stones.

Monkey Army of Ramayana, Nakhon Ratchasima, Thailand

FIGURE 15

According to volkisch (folk) beliefs, Aryans had created a high civilization which existed many millenia ago that was destroyed by either the melting of the ice at the end of the last ice age, or the onset of the ice age, but probably both. The original home of the Aryans was called Thule, at the northernmost reaches of the Earth, the land beyond the northern wind. The term ultima Thule in medieval geographies denotes any distant northern area located beyond the "borders of the known world". Said by Nazi mystics to be the capital of ancient Hyperborea, they placed Ultima Thule in the extreme north near or below Greenland or Iceland. The Thulists believed in the hollow earth theory, with inhabited underground worlds below the icy surface. That once warm country was flooded and iced over, with the advanced race finding underground sanctuary in massive subterranean caverns.

Photo taken by Teobert Maler in the jungles of the Yucatan. A portion of a continuous frieze which surrounded the interior of an underground chamber.

FIGURE 16

The melting occurred rapidly during the final stage of the Pleistocene, from approximately 18,000-11,000 years ago. During this period, there were several changes between glacier advance and retreat. The maximum extent of glaciation within this last glacial period was approximately 22,000 years ago, when sea levels were 400 feet lower world-wide. The melting glaciers which once covered Europe, Canada, and large parts of the earth, were now returning to the ocean and submerging coastlines and islands, forcing the inhabitants to relocate. Their emblem was the swastika.

One of the oldest documented prehistoric symbols is perhaps most famously known as the 'Swastika' in India, but also the 'Fylfot' in England, the 'Hakenkreuz' in Germany, the 'Tetra Gammadion' in Greece, the 'Wan' in China, and the 'Manji' in Japan. In his 1896 book, The Swastika: The Earliest Known Symbol and its Migrations, Thomas Wilson, former cu-

FIGURE 23

rator of the Department of Prehistoric Anthropology in the U.S. National Museum, wrote of the swastika:

An Aryan symbol (卐) used by the Aryan peoples before their dispersion through Asia and Europe. This is a fair subject for inquiry and might serve as an explanation how, as a sacred symbol, the Swastika might have been carried to the different peoples and countries in which we now find it by the splitting up of the Aryan peoples and their migrations and establishment in the various parts of Europe.

Chapter 4

Founded in 1935, the Ahnenerbe was a scientific institute in the Third Reich dedicated to researching the archaeological, linguistic, genetic and cultural history and origins of civilization during the Holocene (our current geological age). According to them, civilizations stemmed from the Aryan survivors of the Pleistocene (ice age). They conducted research, experiments and later launched massive expeditions attempting to rediscover the lost links of Germanic people to their forgotten past, when the Aryan Nordic populations had once ruled the world. Its name came from an obscure German word, 'Ahnenerbe', meaning "inherited from the forefathers."

The scientific contributions of the Ahnenerbe through their historical, anthropological, and archaeological research have been downplayed and ridiculed in the controlled mainstream media (by Rothschild) since the end of WW2.(54) During the entire first half of the twentieth century, while the British and American academics were printing textbooks touting the Piltdawn man (later proven to be a hoax) as the "missing link", the Ahnenerbe were exploring massive pyramids in China, uncovering Caucasoid mummies on the Canary Islands, searching subterranean passages in Tibet, and finding ancient genetic and cultural links between the New World and Europe. While America's top "scholars" were too busy hiding, ignoring, or covering up the many native American mounds, artifacts, earthworks, and out-of-place skeletons found over the centuries, the Ahnenerbe were making our occult (hidden) history public.

All but one member of the Ahnenerbe was released immediately following the war. Most went off to become the top professors in major Universities around the world. They were not criminals, they were the world's brightest researchers in their fields, and what they accomplished was, and largely remains, scientifically valid, unlike what is promoted by the United Nations today in the field of Anthropology. The UN propaganda is little more than a politically motivated falsification of history. Scientific correctness has been replaced by political correctness.

Author Jan van Helsing describes in his book the occult astrotheology held by the Nazis regarding cycles of time and the advent of a new age: the change-over from the Age of Pisces to the Age of Aquarius.(10) According to ancient Indo-Aryan Vedic texts, our solar year, like the twelve revolutions of the moon, was divided into twelve months. Thus the revolution of our sun around the great central sun (the Black Sun of ancient myths) was also divided into twelve parts (ages of the zodiac), which determines the length of the world age. Such a "cosmic month" lasts for 2,155 years, and then changes over to the next age, completing the cycle of a "cosmic year" takes 25,860 years. This is recorded as Plato's Great Year, the precession of the equinox, and also what is referred to as the Mayan long count calander. According organizations, such as the Templars, the next change is not just an ordinary change of the age, but the end of a cosmic year and the start of a whole new cosmic cycle.(10) By completing this 25,860 year cycle, the Earth is transitioning from the age with the weakest cosmic radiation (Pisces) to the age with the strongest (Aquarius). The ancient Aryans defined this current ending cycle we are completing, or Kali Yuga, the age of sin.

According to the this ancient esoteric philosophy, each age change has led to political, religious, social and global geological upheavals of great impact. The precise timing of this change-over from the old age to the new age is called, in Mesopotamian teachings, the three "double steps of Marduk": lasting for 168 years, at the mid-point of which the 'Divine Ray' was expected to reach Earth ushering in change. (10)

In 1894 the Indian astronomer, Sri Yukteswar, wrote that the cause of the precession of the equinox was the result of our sun's orbit around another star (the "Black Sun"). He estimated the orbit period at 24,000 years. This long cycle is the same concept as Plato's Great Year, as well as the Maya Long Count calendar.

The Fixed Cross, consisting of the four constellations, has the same four signs regarded in the Christian belief as the four living creatures of the

FIGURE 53

prophet Ezekiel. These four had the face of a man, Aquarius; the body of a lion, Leo; the horns of an ox, Taurus; and the wings of an eagle, Scorpio. The Eagle was astrologically interchangeable with Scorpio. These same 4 fixed signs of the zodiac are symbolized in the four evangelists, and in the four beasts of Revelations.

Ultima Thule was the name of the capital city of the first surface continent peopled by Aryans. The civilization of this Hyperborean homeland pre-dated both Lemuria and Atlantis. The Scandinavians have a tale of "Ultima Thule", the wonderful land in the high North, where the sun never sets and the ancestors of the Aryan race dwell. Hyperborea was said to be located up in the North Sea and was submerged by rising sea levels since during the ice age. It is said that the Hyperboreans came from a star in the constellation Taurus, and that they were tall, white, blond and blue-eyed. When Hyperborea began to be submerged by water and ice, the Hyperboreans are said to have burrowed huge gigantic tunnels into the Earth's crust and settled under the Himalayan region. The subterranean realm is called Agartha and its capital Shamballah. The ancient Persians call this land "Aryana" the land of origin of the Aryans.

Karl Haushofer claimed that Thule was actually called Atlantis and that the surviving Thule-Atlanteans were separated into two groups, a good one and an evil one. Those who called themselves after their oracle Agharta were the good and settled in the Himalayan region, the evil ones were the Shamballah who wanted to subjugate humanity and they went West. The symbol of Thule, according to Haushofer, was the swastika. He maintained that the fight between the people of Agharta and Shamballah had been going on for many millenia, carried over to the Holocene (present geological age) from the Pleistocene (ice age), when the degraded Atlanteans tried to subjugate and enslave the rest of the civilized world but were thwarted by the Athenians, as recorded by Plato. He saw in the Third Reich the Thule-Gesellschaft; Agharta's representative continuing this ancient conflict against the representatives of Shamballah; the Freemason Zionists. Haushofer was convinced that the land below the Himalayas was the birthplace of the Aryans, which he claimed to have confirmed during his travels in Tibet and India. The head of this subterranean region, he learned, had a representative upon the Earth's surface which was none other than the Dalai Lama. Tibetan lamas and the Dalai Lama personally processed to the Germans that people from Agartha were still living today. According to them, the subterranean land that is anchored in almost all Eastern traditions has spread over thousands of years to areas located under all of the Earth's surface with huge centers under the Sahara desert, the Matto Grosso and the Santa Catarina mountains in Brazil, the Yucatan Peninsula in Mexico, Mount Shasta in California, England, Egypt, and Czechoslovakia.

It seems that Hitler especially sought to discover the entrances to the subterranean world Agartha to get in contact with the descendants of the Aryan "God people" from Alderbaran-Hyperborea. In the myths and traditions of the subterranean world it is often said that the world's surface was yet to suffer a terrible world war (Third World War) which would though be ended by earthquakes, other natural disasters and a switching of the poles and the deaths therefrom of two thirds of humanity. After this

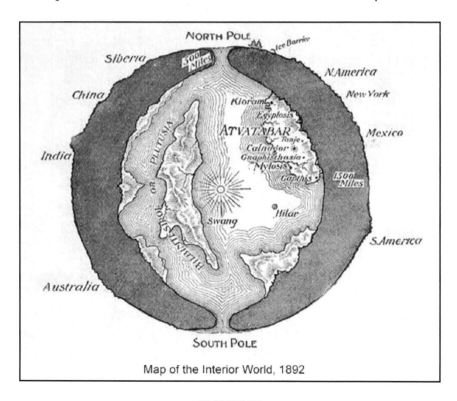

Map of the Interior World, 1892

FIGURE 25

"last war" the several races of the inner earth would reunite with the survivors on the surface and that the thousand-year Golden Age (Aquarian age) would be rung in. Hitler wanted to build an outer "Agartha" or "Aryana" with the Aryan master race, and Germany should be its home. During the existence of the "Third Reich" two large expeditions were sent by the SS to the Himalayas to find those entrances. Further expeditions searched in the Andes, the Matto Grosso mountains in the North and the Santa Catarina mountains in the south of Brazil, in Czechoslovakia and parts of England.

They maintained that the actual life in our planet takes place in the interior, with the master race living inside and the mutants on the surface. This was also said to be a reason why we wouldn't find any life upon other planets of our solar system, as their inhabitants supposedly lived underground. The main entrances seem to always be at the North and South poles. The polar explorer Olaf Jansen and others said that the water in the interior was fresh, which could explain why the ice of the Arctic and Antarctic is made of freshwater, not salt water.(11) It is interesting to note that this view of the make-up of the world is shared and supported by the polar explorers Cook, Peary, Amundsen, Nansen, and Kane and, last but not least, Admiral E. Byrd. All had the same, strange experiences contradicting existing scientific theory. All confirmed that after 76 degrees latitude the winds became warmer, that birds flew north, that they found colored and gray snow which when thawed left colored pollen or volcanic ash. The question arises: where do flower pollen or volcanic ash near the North Pole come from, as not a single volcano is marked on any of the accessible maps? Mammoths were found flash-frozen, whose flesh was still fresh and whose stomach contained undigested buttercups, which grow in semi-tropical climates.

The "weather section" of the Nazi Ahnenerbe (archeological research) headed by Dr. Hans Scultetus, was concentrating on weather forecasts resting on the world-ice cosmology. The Ahnenerbe's forecasts took place over many millenia. Scultetus was interested in the big picture, in knowing how the weather would change over the long term. He wanted to know how the weather on Earth would change when the Sun goddess, to use the volkisch

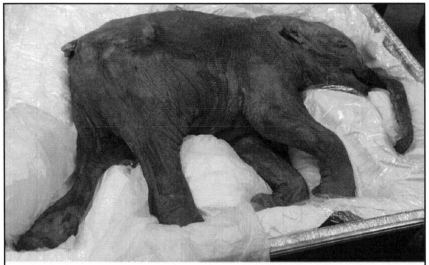

Carcass of perfectly preserved baby woolly mammoth on display

FIGURE 26

analogy, shifted her attention and her golden rays from Earth to that other planet which deserved it more: Mars.

The Nazis believed that the ice at the poles represents the Earth's original state, not its wintry death. The Fire and Ice theory held that it was the Flood, not the ice, that signified the Earth's Last Days. It was an age of evil, and the New Age to be brought in would restore the golden age.

In common with the legendary inhabitants of Atlantis, the Hyperboreans engaged in war with neighboring civilizations. This escalated into the use of atomic weapons, resulting in a pyrrhic victory for the Hyperboreans, who, as well as defeating their enemies, virtually destroyed themselves in the process. The surviving Hyperboreans were soon faced with the prospect of mutated and otherwise radiation damaged offspring. Showing remarkable resolve, those who had not sustained any apparent genetic damage, banded together and effectively removed themselves from the gene pool by relocating underground, a variety of self imposed quarantine.

On the surface, a branch of the descendants of this seminal 'Mother Aryan race' were the proto-Indo-Europeans/Iranians who, like the ripples on a pond, spread out, colonizing various northern areas of the planet after the Deluge, spreading their agricultural civilization and universally recognized swastika symbol. Scotts, Basques, Scandinavians, Guanches, Berbers, Icelanders, Ainu of Japan, Iranian/Indian ruling class, Chinese of the Gobi desert, original Tibetans, Pharaohs of Egypt, proto-Greeks (Hellenes), certain native American, Mesoamerican, and South American tribes; the nobility that established and governed all of these civilizations were of Aryan origin. These disparate nationalities share linguistic patterns, have mythological similarities, and poses at least one common genetic trait; a large percentage of RH-negative blood types. According to the beliefs of the Thule society, a blood characteristic of the Hyperboreans and their extraterrestrial associates. Other races and peoples who posses a rhesus monkey positive blood type (over 80% of the world population) were considered to have gradually become racially impure, as rhesus monkey positive blood (RH+) was thought to be contaminated by generations of contact with the simian-hybridized strands of human DNA.

It is not socially acceptable to attempt to explain human anomalies that do not fit the prevailing "out-of-Africa" model, such as origins of RH negative blood-type. After WW2, the Aryan ideal utopia of a Thule paradise was completely abolished, replaced by an egalitarian utopia promoting a mythical sub-Saharan cradle of civilization, pushed globally with funding by the UN. The "out of Africa" hypothesis backed by the United Nations was universally adopted, often celebrated, and treated as religious dogma in Universities that currently enjoy public federal or state funding and tax exempt status.

It is correctly said that history is always written by the winners, but history is not the only field to have been politically influenced by the victors of the second world war. Many 'conspiracy theorists' claim that there is ongoing technology suppression in the field of free-energy, and that much of the UFO phenomenon, specifically the area of propulsion, is not really as "unidentified" as it is made out to be. An example is the physics behind Die Glocke (German for "The Bell"), a top secret Nazi scientific technological device, secret weapon, or Wunderwaffe.

The Nazi Bell is described as being a device made out of a hard, heavy metal approximately nine feet wide and 12 to 15 feet high, having a shape similar to that of a large bell. This device ostensibly contained two counter-rotating cylinders which would be filled with a mercury-like substance, and cautiously stored in a thermos flask encased in lead. This Die Glocke was further described as emitting strong radiation when activated, an effect that supposedly led to the death of several unnamed Nazi scientists and various plant and animal test subjects. The ruins of a concrete framework, dubbed "The Henge", in the vicinity of the Wenceslas mine (50°37'43?N 16°29'40?E) may have once served as a test rig for an experiment in "anti-gravity propulsion" generated with Die Glocke. Claims have been made by some that the device was considered so important to Hitler that he ordered 60 scientists killed that worked on the project just to guard the technology. Others have speculated that The Nazi Bell was moved, along with other advanced saucer-type craft, to the US as part of a deal made with SS General Hans Kammler, or possibly even ended up in Nazi-friendly South American country like Argentina.

In the 1930's, Nazis exploring the southern extremities of the globe set up a base (called base-211) in Antarctica. You may have heard of Operation Highjump and how Admiral Byrd had an altercation with entrenched German forces that overpowered them with amazing flying craft. A map from the Third Reich (obtained by Russian forces during WW2) has recently surfaced detailing not only the direct passageway used by German U-boats to access this subterranean domain, but also a complete map of both hemispheres of the inner realm of Agartha!

After the Soviet collapse in 1991, the KGB released previously classified files that cast light on the mysterious US led Naval expedition to Antarctica in 1947. The intelligence report, gathered from Soviet KGB spies embedded in the US, revealed that the US Navy had sent the military expedition led by Admiral Byrd to find and destroy a hidden Nazi base. On the way, they encountered and were defeated by a German saucer force that destroyed several ships and planes, forcing the US to retreat and implement a media cover-up lasting up until today. According to author Richard Dolan:

◇◇◇

The Library of Congress adds roughly 60 million pages to its holdings each year, a huge cache of information for the public. However, also each year, the U.S. Government classifies nearly ten times that amount – an estimated 560 million pages of documents. For scholars engaged in political, historical, scientific, or any other archival work, the grim reality is that most of their government's activities are secret." (23)

◇◇◇

Chapter 5

It is correctly said that history is always written by the winners, but written history is not the only field to have been politically influenced by the victors of the Second World War. Many 'conspiracy theorists' claim that there is ongoing technology suppression in the field of free-energy, and that much of the UFO phenomenon, specifically the area of propulsion, is not really as "unidentified" as it is made out to be. An example is the physics behind Die Glocke (German for "The Bell"), a top secret Nazi scientific technological device, secret weapon, or Wunderwaffe.

The Nazi Bell is described as being a device made out of a hard, heavy metal approximately nine feet wide and 12 to 15 feet high, having a shape similar to that of a large bell. This device ostensibly contained two counter-rotating cylinders which would be filled with a mercury-like substance, and cautiously stored in a thermos flask encased in lead. This Die Glocke was further described as emitting strong radiation when activated, an effect that supposedly led to the death of several unnamed Nazi scientists and various plant and animal test subjects. The ruins of a concrete framework, dubbed "The Henge", in the vicinity of the Wenceslas mine (50°37'43?N 16°29'40?E) may have once served as a test rig for an experiment in "anti-gravity propulsion" generated with Die Glocke. Claims have been made by some that the device was considered so important to Hitler that he ordered 60 scientists killed that worked on the project just to guard the technology. Others have speculated that The Nazi Bell was moved, along with other advanced saucer-type craft, to the US as part of a deal made with SS General Hans Kammler, or possibly even ended up in Nazi-friendly South American country like Argentina.

In the 1930's, Nazis exploring the southern extremities of the globe set up a base (called base-211) in Antarctica. You may have heard of Operation Highjump and how Admiral Byrd had an altercation with entrenched German forces that overpowered them with amazing flying craft. A map from the Third Reich (obtained by Russian forces during WW2) has recently surfaced detailing not only the direct passageway used by German U-boats to access this subterranean domain, but also a complete map of both hemispheres of the inner realm of Agartha!

After the Soviet collapse in 1991, the KGB released previously classified files that cast light on the mysterious US led Naval expedition to Antarctica in 1947. The intelligence report, gathered from Soviet KGB spies embedded in the US, revealed that the US Navy had sent the military expedition led by Admiral Byrd to find and destroy a hidden Nazi base. On the way, they encountered and were defeated by a German saucer force that destroyed several ships and planes, forcing the US to retreat and implement a media cover-up lasting up until today.

Officially called, "The US Navy Antarctic Development Program," the naval component of Operation Highjump was comprised of 4700 military personnel, an aircraft carrier (the USS Philippine Sea among the largest of all carriers of the time), and a number of naval support ships and aircraft. The Naval expedition was headed by famed polar explore Admiral Richard Byrd, who had been ordered to: "To consolidate and extend American sovereignty over the largest practical area of the Antarctic continent. To establish Little America."

Byrd's expedition ended after only 8 weeks with "many fatalities" according to initial news reports based on interviews with crew members who spoke to the press while passing through Chilean ports. Rather than deny the heavy casualty reports, Admiral Byrd revealed in an interview that they had encountered a new enemy that "could fly from pole to pole at incredible speeds." Admiral Byrd's statements were published in the Chilean Press but never publicly confirmed by US authorities. Indeed Byrd did not speak again to the Press about Operation Highjump, leaving it for researchers to speculate for decades over what really happened, and why Byrd was silenced.

Indeed, Operation Highjump had suffered "many casualties" as stated in initial press reports from Chile, which may have ended up exposing the first known historical incident involving a battle between US naval forces and an unknown UFO force stationed near Antarctica. It is a historical fact that Nazi Germany devoted significant resources to the exploration of Antarctica, and established a prewar presence there with its first mission in the Antarctic summer of 1938/1939. According to a statement by Grand Admiral Donitz in 1943, "the German submarine fleet is proud of having built for the Führer, in another part of the world, a Shangri-La land, an impregnable fortress." If the fortress was in Antarctica, was it built by the Nazis, or discovered there? After the defeat of Nazi Germany, according various sources, elite Nazi scientists and leaders escaped to this impregnable fortress by Uboats, two of which experienced difficulties and surrendered in Argentina.

In countless biographies of Adolf Hitler's final hours is recounted the act of committing suicide with Eva Braun. He supposedly took a cyanide pill and then shot himself on 30 April 1945, as the Russians bombarded Berlin. A fragment of skull, complete with bullet hole, which was taken from the bunker by the Russians and displayed in Moscow in 2000, appeared to settle the argument. That is, until 2009, when it was genetically tested and shown to have belonged to a 40 year old woman.

According to Connecticut archaeologist and bone specialist Nick Bellantoni, it was clear from the outset that something was amiss. "The bone seemed very thin; male bone tends to be more robust," he said. "And the sutures where the skull plates come together seemed to correspond to someone under 40."(32) In April 1945 Hitler turned 56. The only positive physical proof that Hitler had shot himself had suddenly been rendered worthless.

Could the fallen German dictator, Adolf Hitler, have been among those Nazis who found refuge in South America? To most historians, the idea is preposterous, but the notion that Hitler had fled Europe did not seem preposterous at the time. Many Nazi officials found a warm welcome in Argentina, then led by Juan Peron, a dictator and admirer of Hitler. (32)

Isabelita Peron, the third wife of Juan Peron and President of Argentina, this photo was July 1974 on the occasion of the funeral of Juan Peron.

FIGURE 22

The Argentine Government has still not declassified its files relating to Adolf Hitler, intensifying doubts regarding the official version of Hitler's death. If Hitler had committed suicide, then what could the Argentine files possibly contain that would be worth keeping secret seventy years later?

Chapter 6

Sufis, as a religious sect, have no official country of their own. They do not live in any single geographic region. Instead, they exist throughout the Islamic world as both Shiah and Sunni. Sufis claim to represent the mystical, or esoteric, dimension of Islam which seeks direct and personal knowledge and experience of God. This approach, in many ways, mirrors the mysticism of the Gnostics, as opposed to a strict acceptance of scripture with obedience to the outward laws of orthodox practice. Mohammad (AD 570-632), the founder of the Islamic religion, was said by some of his followers to have members of his entourage as some of the earliest Sufi mystics.

The use of henna in Islam is emphasized by some Muslims as a sunnah, or a behavior learned from the example of Muhammad, which is encouraged but not obligatory. Strong henna traditions often appear in countries that were founded on ancient Aryan civilizations: such as Iran, Afghanistan, and India. The Quran, the holy book of the Islamic faith, does not directly mention henna, but the hadith literature refers to it several times. The hadith literature consists of sayings or anecdotes about Muhammad, as narrated by his companions or followers, compiled mostly during the eighth and ninth centuries. It mentions henna over 20 times, including over ten references to men, including Muhammad himself, using it to color their hair and beards.(42) Muhammad started using red henna to dye his hair in his later years, as he was reported to have been naturally fair-haired hair when he was young. Ibn 'Umar narrates that the Messenger of Allah (Prophet Muhammad) said: "A true believer's dye is yellow, a Muslim's dye is red and a non-believer's dye is black."(42)

Most academic authorities on the issue, who I've found to often times be politically motivated, appear to agree that Muhammad was of a dark complection and hair. However, anthropologist Henric von Schwerin points out: "Red-hair is still honored amongst Moslems as the Prophet Mohammed himself was reported to have red hair." (33)

Jabir reported that the Prophet Muhammad instructed one of his followers with a whitening beard to, 'change it with something and avoid black.' He meant: dye it with a color and do not use black. Islam forbids dying the hair or beard black, but accepts and even venerates yellow and red henna in an aging hair and beard. Shaykh Ahmad Raza Khan in his book Ehkam-e-Shariat writes:

Yellow dyes are good, and in the hadith concerning black dye it states it is of the non-believers. This is unlawful and the ruling of the permissibility is incorrect and void. (42)

There are strands of hair claimed to be from the actual beard of Mohammed on display at a museum in Turkey. Known in Turkish as the Sakal-ı Şerif, the beard was said to have been shaved from Muhammad's face by his favored barber Salman in the presence of Abu Bakr, Ali and several others. Individual hairs were later taken away, but the beard itself is kept protected in a glass container.

This insight into the Aryan cultural and ethnic influence on early Islam helps explain why millions of Muslims today, some being of sub-Saharan African origin with black hair, also dye their beards with red henna. They are following in the foot steps of their prophet, out of imitation and respect, especially during the month of Ramadan, the holy month of fasting. Muhammad was not only naturally ginger or fair-haired, he was also apparently fair-skinned. Umar described the Prophet: "His face was not fat nor rounded; it was white tinged with red."(35)

During her lifetime Aisha, Mohammed's beloved wife, gained the epithet "humayra", a word which has been translated as "light," "reddish," or "fair," but whose meaning is most accurately rendered as "blonde."(36,37,38) She has become known to the Islamic peoples as "Aisha the Blonde." Abu Bakr, Aisha's father, and thus, the father-in-law of Muhammad, was the first Caliph of Islam. He was said to be slenderly built, and dyed his gray beard with red henna in his advanced age.(39) Caliph Ali (AD 656-661), a first cousin and son-in-law of Mohammad, was also renowned for his blond hair, as were his descendants, who founded the Shi'ite branch of Islam. These physical features, which characterized a true descendant of Muhammad, have steadily been visibly lost due to admixture with darker ethnic complications.(37,40) There clearly appears to have been an Aryan element (Haplogroup R1a), amongst the leadership of the Arabic peoples, from the very earliest times. (41)

The esoteric interpretation of the Quran, also called ta'wil, is the allegorical interpretation or the quest for its hidden, or occult, inner meanings. Initially used as a synonym of conventional interpretation, it came to mean a process of discerning its most fundamental understandings.(35) The esoteric interpretations do not usually contradict the conventional (exoteric) interpretations; instead, they discuss the deepest, often secret, hidden and withheld inner levels of spiritual attainment. Sufis practice ancient alchemical techniques, developed long before Islam, which were incorporated into the Islamic faith as mysteries to allow initiated individuals to develop spiritual realization, and then in turn to teach them to others.

Sufis often use music as a means to pray and connect with God, which members achieve by members entering into a group meditative altered state. Although some traditional Islamic leadership frown upon this musical expression, Sufi musical performances, including chanting, dancing, and meditation, aim to lead followers to the subjective experience of annihilation of the ego and the merging with the higher divine self to commune with God directly.

This tradition teaches that the ideal state of self realization is through subsistence, where the mystic is conscious of both a universal unity and, to a lesser degree, of his own individual identity. The goal is to experience a connection to divinity within oneself. What is most essential to Sufism can not be learned intellectually; one can only reach it through personal experience and inward transformation.

The Sufi philosopher, Ibn Arabi, once said that, "When my beloved appears, with what eye do I see him? With his eye, not with mine. For none sees him but himself." It is said that through the heart divinity is most accessible and, according to the mystics, altered states of higher consciousness, psychologically described as an altered trance state, are ritualistically entered into in an effort to embrace and experience this spiritual union.

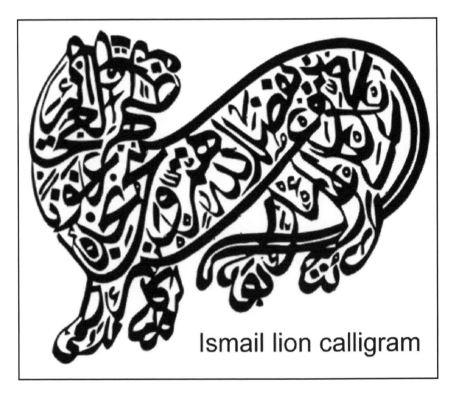

Ismail lion calligram

FIGURE 31

Eventually the Sufis gathered and aggregated alchemical and Gnostic teachings from various ancient sources and, combining them, established numerous new synthetic mystery school traditions - an amalgamation of alchemical wisdom derived from India, Egypt, Persia and Greece. One such mystery tradition, called the House of Wisdom, was founded in Cairo. Many seeking ancient knowledge came from around the Middle East and Asia to study at this mystery school, which was divided into nine degrees leading to enlightenment. Adepts who graduated from the House of Wisdom went on to found their own mystery schools. Hassani Sabbah, nicknamed the 'Old Man', or 'Lord of the Mountain' formed one such school, called the School of the Hashishi ("Assassins").

Chapter 7

The 'Old Man' Hassan Sabbah, also known as 'Lord of the Mountain', formed an elite secret society called the School of the Hashishi ("Assassins"). A popular theory links the word 'Hashish' (can-

Archaeological remains of the Alamut Fortress in Iran

FIGURE 20

nabis) to the word 'Hashishin', implying that they were named after the hash that they consumed. Unlike alcohol, Islam did not prohibit cannabis. Another hypothesis for the name stems from 'Assasseen', which in Arabic means 'Guardians', and some scholars have considered this to be the true origin of the word Assassin: 'Guardians of the Secrets'. (33)

In Persia (modern Iran), from the highest recesses (2163 meters above sea level) of the thousand year-old impenetrable mountain fortress of Alamut, meaning "Eagle's Nest", Sabbah the Lord of the Mountain directed a covert brotherhood of fearless hashish smoking warriors who were completely dedicated to his undisclosed cause, willing to carry out his every order and, if necessary, die for him willingly and without hesitation. (46)

Benjamin of Tudela said: "He is their Elder, and upon his command all of the men of the mountain come out or go in, they are believers of the word of their elder and everyone everywhere fears them, because they even kill kings."(47)

Born in the Persian city of Qom in the 1050's, Hassani Sabbah preached absolute devotion to a transcendental God. The family who raised him were from a Shi'ah sect known as the Twelvers. The term "Twelver" refers to its adherents' belief in twelve divinely ordained leaders, known as the Twelve Imams, and in the Mahdi ("guided one"), who will return as the redeemer of Islam and who will rule the world, ridding it of evil. People of the Twelver faith form majorities, or significant minorities, in Iran, Iraq, Azerbaijan, Bahrain, Lebanon, Kuwait, India, Bangladesh, Pakistan, Afghanistan, Qatar, United Arab Emirates, Saudi Arabia, Oman, Yemen, Egypt, and Uzbekistan. Alevis in Turkey and Albania, based on Sufi elements of the Bektashi Order, and Alawis in Syria, also share belief in the Twelve Imams. There is also a branch of Shia Islam whose adherents are known as Seveners. They differ from the Twelvers in the identity of their appointed spiritual successor (Imam), who possesses special political authority over their community.(35)

The Bektashi Sufi Order shared the esoteric belief in the twelve Imams, and was very influential and widespread in the Ottoman Empire, having numerous lodges scattered throughout Anatolia. The kept their core beliefs

Painting depicting the 12 Imams

FIGURE 32

secret from outsiders and non-initiated Muslims. Hassani Sabbah was well versed in these same core inner alchemical secrets.

Within his mountain fortress of Alamut, Lord Sabbah built the legendary 'Garden of Earthly Delights' which would play an important role in the initiation rites of the Assassins. The garden lay peacefully secluded in a beautiful valley nestled between two high mountains. Here he had imported exotic plants, birds that few had ever seen before, and unusual animals from all over the world. Luxurious palaces of marble and gold, decorated with beautiful paintings and fine silk furniture, surrounded the lush gardens. Streams of milk, wine, and honey flowed throughout this earthly paradise, while fountains gushed with wine or pure spring water. (33, 46)

Lord Sabbah gave his initiates spiked food and drink, and after the powerful potion of opium and hashish knocked them out, they would be carried into the sacred garden while in a deep sleep. When an initiate awoke from his slumber, a host of young beautiful houris ("virgins") would greet him, singing and dancing and playing lovely flutes and other instruments for him.(45) As Robert Anton Wilson describes it:

"Welcome to paradise," they sang as the awakening initiate gazed about in wonder. "By the magic of the holy Lord Hassan, you have entered Paradise while still alive." And they fed him exotic imported "paradise fruit", far sweeter and stranger than the local fruit he had known before, and they showed him the animals of paradise (imported from as far away as Japan, in some cases), creatures far more remarkable than those ordinarily seen in their local region. (45)

The initiate would be covertly fed more hashish and opium during the experience to ensure the maximum effect on his psyche. Then, as the young man sat entranced by the beauty and wonder of 'heaven', as described by Robert Anton Wilson:

The houris (young virgins) finished the dance, and nude and splendid as they were, rushed forward in a bunch, like flowers cast before the wind. And some fell at the candidate's feet and kissed his ankles; some kissed knees or thighs, one sucked raptly at his penis, others kissed the chest and arms and belly, a few kissed eyes and mouth and ears. And as he was smothered in this hashish-in-

The Dream of the Believer c.1870 by Achille Zo

FIGURE 33

tensified avalanche of love, the lady working on his penis sucked and sucked and he climaxed in her mouth "as softly and slowly and blissfully as a single snowflake falling. (33)

◇◇

After more opium was introduced and began to flow into the bloodstream, the young candidate slept again; and in their torpor, they were removed from the Garden of Delights and returned to the banquet hall of Lord Hassan. There they awoke, and after pledging their devotion, became one of the illuminated. This technique proved effective. Hassan could demand absolute loyalty from his followers, with no questions asked. Another version of the story comes to us via Marco Polo, from his visit to Alamut in 1273:

◇◇

The Old Man kept at his court such boys of twelve years old as seemed to him destined to become courageous men. When the Old Man sent them into the garden in groups of four, ten or twenty, he gave them hashish to drink. They slept for three days, then they were carried sleeping into the garden where he had them awakened. When these young men woke, and found themselves in the garden with all these marvelous things, they truly believed themselves to be in paradise. And these damsels were always with them in songs and great entertainments; they received everything they asked for, so that they would never have left that garden of their own will. And when the Old Man wished to kill someone, he would take him and say: 'Go and do this thing. I do this because I want to make you return to paradise'. And the assassins go and perform the deed willingly.

◇◇

This was only a small part of Hassan's system, which he had divided into levels or degrees. The Assassins combined both the exoteric and esoteric doctrines of Sufi Islam. Sabbah was a noted alchemist, so part of

Depiction of Hassan-i Sabbah at Alamut

FIGURE 34

the curriculum for future Assassins involved mastering occult methods for reaching higher planes of consciousness.

Of course, they also learned how properly to kill a man with poison or a dagger. Initiates learned multiple languages, as well as the dress and manners of merchants, monks and soldiers. Moreover, they learned to fake the beliefs and devotions of every major religion. In this way, an Assassin could pretend to be anyone from a well-to-do merchant to a Sufi mystic, a Christian, or a common soldier.

The Assassins persisted for over 100 years after Sabbah's death, but Halaku Khan, son of Ghengis Khan, finally sieged and conquered Alamut in 1256. Sabbah's chief minister was ordered to write a complete history of the Assassins (based on records in the Alamut library) and this is work supplies most of the historical data about the order.

During the Crusades, the Assassins fought both for and against the Crusaders, likely whichever suited their agenda. As a result of the contact, the Crusaders brought back to Europe the Assassin's system, which numerous secret societies in the West would adopt or mimic. The Knights Templars, the Society of Jesus, Priory de Sion, the Freemasons, the Rosicrucians, etc., all owe their organizational efficiency to the old man Hassan. In fact, the Illuminati had their origins in the mystical aspect of the Assassin order, although most equate the Illuminati with the Bavarian Illuminati, a revised version of the Assassin system. (46) Even our modern Assassination cults (FBI, CIA, MOSSAD, etc.) have incorporated many of the Assassin's techniques into their methodologies. In a CIA training manual titled "Study of Assassination" contains traces of the Assassin influence through-out. The document even mentions Hasan Sabbah by name. The Mossad former motto also happens to be: "By Way of Deception, Thou Shalt Do War."

Another Sufi sect that are part of the mystery tradition are the Yezidis. They currently occupy a small territory in northern Iraq and claim they can trace their history back 6,000 years, many millenia before Islam. Contributing to the Sumerian, Babylonian, and Assyrian civilizations, the Yezidis are mystics who practice a synthetic mystery school which, at the time of the Knights Templars, had settlements in Syria and may have interacted with and influenced the Templars.

The Knights Templar learned how to create a mystery school from these Sufis cults. When the Knights Templars arrived in the Middle East, the Sufis had already established numerous mystery schools which were a synthesis of those of the ancient world. The Templars created their own synthetic mystery school known as the Holy Grail mystery school. They wove into this mystery school much of the alchemical wisdom they had learned from the various Sufi traditions, as well as esoteric wisdom from the Kabbalah and both the Greek and Egyptian mystery schools.

Baron Rudolf von Sebottendorff founded the Thule Gesellschaft, an occult organization that would eventually have strong ties to the Nazis, however, left for Turkey when the organization was adopted by Hitler's regime making it political.

In his book originally published in Germany in 1924, *Secret Practices of the Sufi Freemasons: The Islamic Teachings at the Heart of Alchemy,*

FIGURE 35

he purports to deliver inner Masonic practices from the Bektashi Order of Sufis. The book is mainly an esoteric interpretation of Masonic hand signs, but it includes the abbreviated letters found at the beginnings of some of the Quran's chapters, Arabic letter mysticism, and vowel chanting. (2) He claims that the basic idea of this sect is that God reveals himself in the "Word", which is made up of sounds, or letters with accompanying numerical values. These are made manifest in the human body through certain exercises that, he claims, make up the essential components at the heart of alchemy. In this context, the word alchemy refers not to the art of converting base metals, but to spiritual alchemy, the transformation of the individual soul.

The almost qigong-like exercises Sebottendorff presents make up a lengthy initiatory routine based around Bektashi internal alchemy. By combining four Masonic hand signs, one of which Sebottendorff says is now lost to western Masonry, with the intonation of specific vowels and accompanying movement, the practitioner transforms himself into a spiritual being in an alchemical process designed to burn away the dross of humanity and realize the divine in human nature. In the words of von Sebottendorf:

These exercises are characterized by the use of the three signs or recognition, employed by modern Freemasons: sign, grip and word - except these are not signs of recognition, not mere symbols in the best case, but rather magical operations designed to induct the finer radiation of the primordial power - to incorporate them into the body and thereby make the body more spiritual, to give the balance of power to the spirit over the body. (2)

FIGURE 36

He explains that these practices are Rosicrucian and that Oriental Freemasonry preserved much of the ancient doctrines of wisdom, which modern Freemasonry has forgotten:

Modern Free-masonry, which since the Constitution of 1717 was developed into worldwide Freemasonry, both is and is not the continuation of the old Freemasonry of the Middle Ages. It is so as far as outward appearances are concerned, but as it concerns the nature and content of the teaching it has entirely abandoned the ways of ancient Masonry. (2)

Perhaps the most interesting feature of this Masonic qi gong is that Sebottendorff claims that, if taken seriously and performed with due diligence and faith, it is risk free, even if you might feel like you wasted some time. That said, the entire practice can take over a year, although it requires relatively little amount of time each day to perform. The ancient formulas are thought to incorporate spiritual power into the body, and to transform the soul from its base state into a noble, god-like state: the Magnum Opus of the medieval alchemists.(2)

The Knights Templar adopted these inner alchemy techniques and the European Freemasons preserved them. Still part of the Masonic mysteries, these Sufi spiritual practices have the goal of transforming the practitioner along the lines of Masonic moral allegory. But where did the Sufis learn?

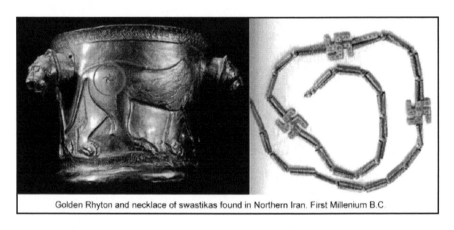

Golden Rhyton and necklace of swastikas found in Northern Iran. First Millenium B.C.

FIGURE 37

The Medes were a people of Indo-Iranian (Aryan) origin who inhabited the western and north-western portion of present-day Iran. By the 6th century BC (prior to the Persian invasion) the Medes had established an empire that stretched from Aran (the modern-day Republic of Azerbaijan) to Central Asia and Afghanistan. Today's population of the western part of the Iranian Plateau (including many Persian-speakers, Kurds and Azeris) consider themselves their descendents.

Apart from a few personal names, the original Aryan language of the Medes is almost entirely unknown, but it was most likely similar to the

Avestan and Scythian languages (proto-Indo-European/Iranian). Herodotus mentions that: "The Medes had exactly the same equipment as the Persians; and indeed the dress common to both is not so much Persian as Median."(7)

Eventually, the older tribes of Aryan Iran lost their distinct character and amalgamated into one people, the Iranians. In Arabic texts, as in the Greco-Roman tradition, Zoroaster is the "founder" of the Magians, Arabic 'Majusya'. There are many views on the timeline for Zoroaster's life. The traditional Zoroastrian date for Zarathushtra's birth and ministry is around 600 B.C. Greek sources placed him as early as 6000 BC. Zoroaster spoke

Robert Sepehr, Pergamon Museum, Berlin, Germany.

FIGURE 38

of duality and ceasing balance at the end of time; his goal, was to show humans their connection to one source of light and consciousness. According to the Zend Avesta, the sacred book of Zoroastrianism, Zoroaster was born in Azerbaijan, in northern Persia (just north of modern Iran). (12)

A Magus was a Zoroastrian astrologer-priest from ancient Persia, and was also referred to as a sorcerer or wizard. The terms magic and magician derive from the word "magus." The English term may also refer to a shaman. The Greek word is attested from the 5th century B.C., as a direct loan from the Old Persian "magus." (7)

Professor of Chinese at the University of Pennsylvania, Victor H. Mair, provides archaeological and linguistic evidence suggesting that the Chinese "wu" (shaman; witch, wizard; magician) was also a loanword from the Old Persian *magus "magician; magi":

The recent discovery at an early Chou site of two figurines with unmistakably Caucasoid or Europoid feature is startling prima facie evidence of East-West interaction during the first half of the first millennium Before the Current Era. It is especially interesting that one of the figurines bears on the top of his head the clearly incised graph (cross with potents) which identifies him as a "wu" (shaman; witch, wizard; magician).(40)

The Aryan, or Indo-European, root appears to have expressed power or ability. This meaning continued, e.g. in Greek "mekhos" (see mechanics) and in Germanic magan (English may), magts (English might, the expression "might and magic"). The original significance of the name for the Median priests, thus, seems to have been "the powerful". The modern Persian "Mobed" derived from an Old Persian compound magu-pati "lord priest".

The plural "Magi" entered the English language ca. 1200, referring to the Magi mentioned in Matthew 2:1. The singular following only consider-

Persian Bas-relief from Persepolis

FIGURE 39

ably later, in the late 14th century, when it was borrowed from Old French in the meaning magician together with magic.

In Farsi, Magi is 'meguceen', which meaning "Fire Worshipper," and it is the origin of the word "magician". While, in Herodotus, "Magos" refers to either an ethnically Aryan member of one of the tribes/peoples (ethnous) of the Medes, or to one of the Persian priests who could interpret dreams, it could also be used for any enchanter or wizard. (38, 39)

In Hellenism, "Magos" started to be used as an adjective, meaning "magical", as in magas techne "ars magica" (e.g. used by Philostratus). Sources from before the Hellenistic period include Xenophon, who had first-hand experience at the Persian Achaemenid court. In his early 4th century BC Cyropaedia, Xenophon depicts the Magians as authorities for all religious matters, and imagines the Magians were responsible for the education of the emperor-to-be.(39)

According to Robert Charles Zaehner, author of the book, *The Dawn and Twilight of Zoroastrianism:*

We hear of Magi not only in Persia, Parthia, Bactria, Chorasmia, Aria, Media, and among the Sakas, but also in non-Iranian lands like Samaria and Egypt. Their influence was also widespread throughout Asia Minor. It is, therefore, quite likely that the sacerdotal caste of the Magi was distinct from the Median tribe of the same name.(38)

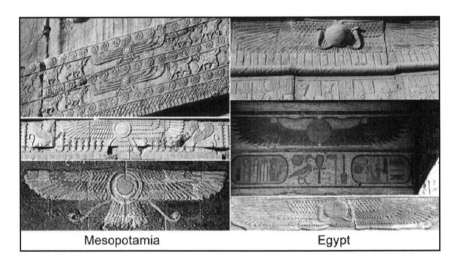

Mesopotamia   Egypt

FIGURE 40

William Wynn Westcott was an English coroner, ceremonial magician, Theosophist and Freemason, who was extremely influential in the latter part of the 19th century. He was a Supreme Magus (chief) of the Rosicrucian Society of England and went on to co found the Golden Dawn. An expert in Kabbalah, Westcott's book, *The Occult Power of Numbers,* explains that:

The followers of Pythagoras referred every object, planet, man, idea, and essence to some number or other, in a way which to most moderns must seem curious and mystical in the highest degree. 'The numerals of Pythagoras', says Porphyry, who lived about 300 A.D., 'were hieroglyphic symbols, by means whereof he explained all ideas concerning the nature of things', and the same [numeric] method of explaining the secrets of nature is once again being insisted upon in the new revelation of the 'Secret Doctrine', by H.P. Blavatsky. Numbers are a key to the ancient views of cosmogony - in its broad sense, spiritually as well as physically considered, to the evolution of the present human race; all systems of religious mysticism are based upon numerals. The sacredness of numbers begins with the Great First Cause, the One, and ends only with the nought or zero: symbol of the infinite and boundless universe.(36)

The Enlightened Magi of every age have been able to pass down their occult Gnostic knowledge or 'Divine Wisdom' (Sophia), despite political persecution, by using the language of numbers which is at the core of the alchemical mysteries. St Augustine, an early Christian theologian and philosopher, stated that: "Numbers are the thoughts of God. The Divine Wisdom is reflected in the numbers impressed on all things, the construction of the physical and moral world alike is based on eternal numbers."(37)

Occult researcher, lecturer and author, David Icke, admirably articulates the hidden significance embedded in numbers, which all secret societies and ancient mystery schools have venerated through the ages until today. In Icke's words:

These number codes have even deeper meanings than the more obvious ones of days, months, and the zodiac. Numbers also represent vibrational frequencies. Every frequency resonates to a certain number, color and sound. Some frequencies, represented by numbers, colors and sounds, are particularly powerful. Symbols also represent frequencies and they affect the subconscious without the person realizing it is happening. This is another reason why certain symbols are seen in secret societies, national flags, company logos, and advertising.(41)

In his book, *The Atlantis Encyclopedia*, author Frank Joseph turns to Plato in search of an explanation for the deeper meaning held in symbols and numbers, such as the pentagram and hexagram; the five and six pointed star respectively. Frank points out that Plato attributed the occult significance all the way back to the time of Atlantis:

In Kritias, Plato wrote that the numbers 5 and 6 were sacred in Atlantis, where they were encoded in architecture, art, and ceremonial life 'to honor the odd and even days.' "The Atlanteans' choice of these numerals reflects their holistic religion, the 'Navel of the World,' whose adherents strove for spiritual synthesis and balance. The number 5 represents the male principle of conscious outward action, while 6 stands for female intuitive receptivity. (42)

William W. Westcott's book, *Numbers: Their Occult Power and Mystic Virtues,* diligently describes and tabulates common numeric themes in religions and mythology. It says the following about the sacred number twelve:

In Scandinavia, the Great Odin had 12 names personified attributes. The Kabalists esteem the 12 permutations of the Tetragrammaton, In an ordinary pack of Playing Cards there are 12 Court Cards (but the Tarot Pack also has 4 Cavaliers). There were 12 Appearances of Jesus after his death. In the Bible there were 12 tribes of Israel, 12 brothers of Joseph, 12 judges of Israel, 12 great patriarchs, 12 old testament prophets, 12 kings of Israel, 12 princes of Israel, and Jesus' 12 disciples. 12 signs of the zodiac, the 12 months of the year, the 12 hours of day and 12 hours of night. We also have 12 days of Christmas, 12 grades in school, 12 step programs, 12 jurors, 12 notes before the octave, 12 eggs in a dozen, 12 inches in a foot, Majestic12, and 12 years of childhood (before the 7 teen years start) and the Jewish Barmitsfa at 13. (43)

This is the sacred 12 and one as some people describe it, and it is one major reason why the numbers 12 and 13 keep recurring. Wescott goes on to associate the number 12 with the 12 houses of the zodiac, which the Sun (represented by number 13) passes through on it's journey through the ecliptic, which is the basis for the field known as Astrotheology. In his words once again:

♦♦♦♦♦♦♦♦♦♦♦♦♦♦♦♦♦♦♦♦♦♦♦♦♦♦♦♦♦♦

A common theme in all mystery school traditions is of 12 disciples, knights or followers surrounding a deity. The number 12 is a code, among other things, for the 12 months of the year and the houses of the zodiac through which symbolically travels the Sun, the 'god', symbolized as 13. (43)

♦♦♦♦♦♦♦♦♦♦♦♦♦♦♦♦♦♦♦♦♦♦♦♦♦♦♦♦♦♦

Thirteen represents the moon and the female lunar energy, the essence of which has long been silenced by the powers that exclusively promote religiously patriarchal Sun/Son worship. This is why 13, in popular culture, is an unlucky number. The 13th floor will often be left out of the building design, omitted from the elevator. Or the 13th street will be omitted, as is the case in Santa Monica, California, where 13th street (between 12th and 14th Street) is replaced by a street called Euclid, after the famous Mathematician/Alchemist. It is meant to be unlucky for you, the profane, but not for the initiated elites who understand its mystical qualities.

FIGURE 41

Author Elizabeth van Buren gives another Kabbalistic example of the sacred respect, and reverence for numbers: "The rabbis of old believed that through the uses and permutations of the numbers 5, 6, and 10, the sum of which is 21, or 3 times 7 (again the Trinity and the Septenary), total knowledge of the universe could be gained." (37)

According to Herodotus, the Magi were not simply the sacred Kabbalists and a (Gnostic) priest caste of the Medes; they helped to organize Persian society after the fall of Assyria and Babylon.

Robert Sepehr, Ishtar gate, Pergamon Museum, Berlin, Germany.

FIGURE 42

Cyrus the Great, the founder of the Persian Empire, and his son Cambyses II, curtailed the political power and influence of the Magi. The Magi revolted against Cambyses, and set up a rival claimant to the throne, one of their own, who took the name of Smerdis. The Persians, under Darius I, defeated Smerdis and his forces. The minority sect of the Magi continued in Persia, but with limited influence after this political setback.

During the Classical era (555 BCE - 300 CE), some Aryan-Magi migrated westward, settling in Greece, and then Italy. For more than a century, Mithraism, a religion derived from Persia, was the largest single religion in Rome. The Magi were likely involved.

Faravahar relief in Persepolis, Iran

FIGURE 43

After invading Arabs succeeded in taking Ctesiphon in 637, Islam replaced Zoroastrianism, and the power of the Magi faded. Much of their Gnostic and alchemical secrets were kept alive, however, via the Sufis. The Knights Templars transferred the esoteric teachings into the European lodges, such as the Rosicrucian.

Chapter 8

The definition of Gnosis and its proper context as it was used in ancient times is a feminine Greek noun, which literally means "knowledge". In the Hellenistic era the term became associated with the mystery cults and was used to describe an intuitive wisdom, as opposed to a common, externally derived intellectual knowledge.(49) It was the divine wisdom and esoteric knowledge of spiritual truth essential to salvation. Philo of Alexandria was a Hellenistic Jewish philosopher who refers to the "knowledge" (Gnosis) and "wisdom" (Sophia) of God.(50)

The Greek noun Sophia is translated into "wisdom".(49) In Christian, Islamic, or Jewish mysticism, and Gnosticism 'Gnosis' signifies a spiritual knowledge, in the sense of mystical enlightenment or divine insight.(24) In this spiritual context, Gnosis emerges directly from the inside, such as an inner voice, gut feeling, or conscience; not dependent on any data from one's outside environment. According to Gnostic philosophy, a vast ocean of this divine wisdom lays latent within each person, which through specific application of ancient alchemical practices can be harnessed and accessed.

The processes of this inner-alchemy may employ certain natural substances, and special disciplines to purify and transform the physical body;

as well as the mind and soul. The stated goal of these sacred and guarded practices is nothing less than to literally evolve the person's consciousness

Manly P. Hall

FIGURE 44

and being into a higher state of existence. This would include the attainment of certain mystical abilities, such as clairvoyance, heightened intuition, astral 'vision', etc. The Knights Templars likely acquired their secrets of Gnosis, internal-alchemy and the Kabbalah from several different sources during their nearly 200 years in the middle east.

Though the true origin of the Kabbalah is in dispute, in his book, *The Secret Teachings of all Ages*, the respected scholar of the occult, Manly P. Hall, says:

While the greatest, minds of the Jewish and Christian worlds have realized that the Bible is a book of allegories, few seem to have taken the trouble to investigate its symbols and parables. When Moses instituted his Mysteries, he is said to have given to a chosen few initiates certain oral teachings which could never be written but were to be preserved from one generation to the next by word-of-mouth transmission. Those instructions were in the form of philosophical keys, by means of which the allegories were made to reveal their hidden significance. These mystic keys to their sacred writings were called by the Jews the Qabbalah (Cabala, Kaballah).(27)

Many of the Knights Templar's deepest Kabbalistic secrets of the religious mysteries were likely learned from the Sufis, the mystical adepts of

Islam, who were among the greatest alchemists of their era. The Sufis had acquired and retained much of their ancient alchemical traditions, including the Kabbalah, from traveling throughout Persia (Iran), Turkey, and the rest of the Muslim empire, which once stretched from Spain to India.

FIGURE 27

The Templars also received their guarded teachings from lineages of Gnostic masters that claimed to have descended directly from the time of Jesus. There are said to be two lineages/churches which were established after the crucifixion: one lineage was founded upon St. Peter and it became the Catholic church, the other lineage was founded upon Mary Magdalene becoming the Gnostic lineage in Christianity. Effectively suppressed for centuries, a group of "Gnostic Gospels" were discovered in the Egyptian desert in 1945, now known as the Nag Hammadi library. The collection of thirteen ancient codices containing over fifty texts have been slowly translated in the years since they were first uncovered. This immensely important discovery includes texts once thought to have been entirely destroyed during the early Christian struggle to define orthodoxy. (28)

Scriptures such as the *Gospel of Thomas*, the *Gospel of Philip*, and the *Gospel of Truth* have provided impetus to a major re-evaluation of early Christian history and the role of the 'divine feminine', the female aspect of God; blatantly excluded from the official canon. These texts also reveal that Mary Magdalene may actually have been a very close disciple and companion of Jesus who, at times, was taught Gnostic wisdom that all the other apostles were not.(28)

Nag Hammadi library

FIGURE 28

The Templars clearly had a very special relationship with Mary Magdalene and, in fact, venerated her as one of their Patroness. While in areas of the middle east, especially around Phoenicia, the early Templars were exposed to interpretations about Mary that was not being taught publicly in Europe. They learned that she had been a very prominent member of a lineage of ancient adepts passed down until the time of the Crusade, when the Templars are said to have become its guardian.

The core teaching of the Gnostic church is said to be about accessing the intuitive wisdom that lays latent within all people. The Templars recognized Mary as an incarnation of both the goddess Sophia and of Venus, the goddess of love. The Latin name Venus also corresponds perfectly to the Aryo-Germanic Freya, Fenus, and Fenussin. This should not be surprising since they stem from the Aryan proto-language itself in which Latin, Greek, English, Farsi, Sanskrit, German, etc., are rooted and thus all mythological names and concepts can be interpreted by means of this mother language.

As Sophia, Mary embodied the essence of Gnostic wisdom. As Venus, Mary held the keys of the attracting power that is required for success in

Mary Magdalene, St. Johns' Cathedral in Toruń

FIGURE 29

all alchemical experiments. Because Mary was both Sophia and Venus to the Templars, it is said that they came to call upon her wisdom for success in all of their Gnostic and alchemical practices. The Templars practiced

Similarities in Vocabulary Indicating Close Relationships between Select Indo-European (Aryan) Languages

English	German	Spanish	Greek	Latin	Sanskrit
father	vater	padre	pater	pater	pitar
one	ein	uno	hen	unus	ekam
fire	feuer	fuego	pyr	ignis	agnis
field	feld	campo	agros	ager	ajras
sun	sonne	sol	helios	sol	surya
king	könig	rey	basileus	rex	raja
god	gott	dios	theos	deus	devas

USA	Germany	Spain	Greece	Italy	India

FIGURE 30

sex magick, and the Goddess represented this method of attaining divine wisdom. Snakes and owls were also venerated symbols, which represented Gnostic wisdom. In Greek mythology, a miniature Owl baby (Athene noctua) traditionally represents or accompanies Athena, the virgin goddess of wisdom, or Minerva, her incarnation in Roman mythology.(51) The actual reasons behind the association of Athena and the owl are lost in time. Some mythographers, such as David Kinsley and Martin P. Nilsson suggest that she may descend from a Minoan palace goddess associated with birds. (52)

Snake Goddess figurines, found by the British archaeologist Arthur Evans in 1903, of a woman with an owl perched atop her head and holding a snake in each hand have been excavated from Minoan archaeological sites in Crete dating from approximately 1600 BC.

Some scholars relate the snake goddess with the Phoenician Goddess Astarte, whose worship was connected with drug use and orgiastic sex cults. Her temples were usually decorated with serpentine motifs. In

Minoan Snake Goddess, Crete (1600 BCE).

FIGURE 45

a related Greek myth Europa, who is often identified with Astarte in ancient sources,(29) was a Phoenician princess who Zeus abducted and carried to Crete. (30) Arthur Evans linked the Phoenician snake goddess with the Egyptian snake goddess Wadjet. Statuettes similar to the "snake goddess" identified as *priest of Wadjud* and *magician* were found in Egypt. (31)

The Knights Templars also came to venerate the Black Madonna, which to them, represented both the attractive power of Venus, as well as the hidden secret wisdom of Sophia. This helps to better understand why the Templars brought back numerous Black Madonnas with them from the Holy land, building grand Gothic cathedrals around them in Europe, always dedicated to Mary.

The Black Madonnas were set on the main alters of these cathedrals and enhanced the purpose of these great buildings, which was to generate the 'holy spirit' power of the goddess.

The Templars infused sacred geometrical principals to design buildings that were conductive to spiritual energy. Such building are essentially designed as alchemical crucibles; places where alchemy is said to constantly occur and amplify within those who observe prayer and participate in other types of spiritual work. If you visit a Gothic cathedral today, there's a good chance you'll see stain-glass windows decorated with motifs centered around the goddess symbol of the rose, or an actual Black Madonna relic.

The Templars supposedly discovered how to access their innate intuitive wisdom (Sophia) or Gnosis through the diligent practice of tantric

FIGURE 46

yoga and deep trance meditation, as well as other traditional alchemical techniques part of the Goddess spiritual traditions that encourages its followers to find their answers through direct experience with the divinity inside themselves. The Goddess path to enlightenment is still strong throughout the world and is practiced among Shamans, Gnostics, Yogis, Wiccans, Mystics, Kabbalists, and Pagans.

The Goddess tradition is also known as the Teaching of the Rose. The rose is a symbol of the Goddess, as well as for alchemy and gnosis, which are branches of the ancient goddess spiritual tradition. The rose was used as a symbol for Mary, as it was also used as an ancient symbol of Venus. The

Goddess Venus was said to rule over the attracting power of love, and Mary was recognized as a personification of love.

One of the titles of the Templars was Knights of the Rose Cross. When the secret societies of Europe acquired the Gnostic and alchemical wisdom of the Knights Templars, many also adopted Mary as their patroness and the rose as their symbol. An example of another popular alchemical sect that shares the symbol of the rose are the Rosecrucians, meaning 'those of the rose cross'. These various hidden societies became collectively known as sub-Rosa. That is to say, they existed under the symbol of the rose.

FIGURE 47

Although it is a widely held belief that these secretive groups were exclusively created to protect Mary's sacred bloodline, which may also be true, it was the secret alchemical tradition that she was a patroness of which was actually being so closely guarded for so many centuries. That is not to say there is no such bloodline in existence, but merely that this was not the singular or primary concern, in this author's humble opinion, of the Templars efforts.

In the Holy land, the Templars learned many of the mysteries from the Sufis, who in tern learned from earlier Goddess cults of the Babylonian Ishtar, and still earlier Sumerian Inanna.

In pre-Islamic times, Mecca was founded to be a shrine to the Goddess. The Black Stone of Kaaba in Mecca, towards which Muslims still pray in the center of the Grand Mosque in Mecca today, is set in large solid silver mountings which on whole resembles the vulva of the goddess.

The Kaaba is accurately aligned on two heavenly phenomena: the cycles of the moon and the rising of Canopus, the brightest star after Sirius. Pre-Islamic worship of the goddess seems to be primarily associated with Al'Lat, which simply means 'goddess'. She is a triple goddess, similar to the Greek lunar deity Kore/Demeter/Hecate. Each aspect of this trinity corresponds to a phase of the moon. Islamic traditions continue to recognize these three, but labels them 'daughters of Allah'.

In pre-Muslim times, the goddess's temple at Mecca was preeminent, whether to celebrate life, ask protection, or pray for offspring. Legend tells how Abraham, unable to produce children by his wife Sarah, came here to make love to his slave Hagar. When Mohammed wanted to supplant Al'Lat with Allah, this was the one Temple that he had to conquer. Although Mohammed did conquer the Kaaba, little else changed. The faithful still circle the Holy Kaaba seven times, as was the tradition. (25)

Deities of other cultures known to have been associated with black stones include Aphrodite at Paphos, Cybele at Pessinus and later Rome, Astarte at Byblos and the famous Artemis/Diana of Ephesus. At Mecca, the Goddess was haybah or Sheba the Old Woman, which was worshiped as a black aniconic stone like the Goddess of the Scythian Amazons.

The sacred Black Stone that now enshrines in the Kaaba was her feminine symbol, marked by the sign of the yoni (vagina), and covered like the ancient Mother by a veil. The Black Stone rests in the Haram, "Sanctuary", cognate of "harem," which used to mean a Temple of Women, in Babylon, a shrine of the Goddess Har, mother of harlots. Hereditary guardians of the

Haram were the Koreshites, "children of Kore", Mohammed's own tribe. The holy office was originally held by women, before it was taken over by male priests calling themselves eni Shayban ("Sons of the Old Woman").(25)

Yoni symbol of the Goddess

FIGURE 48

Various Classical writers describe the sexual rituals which went on in the honor of the ancient Goddess - which include the practice which is now known by the disdainful term of 'sacred prostitution'. Knowledge of ancient rites, as well as the transmutation of sexual energy, was retained through the ages and not completely eradicated by the arrival of Patriarchal religions.

The Sufis taught the Knights Templars that the goal of internal alchemy was to awaken the divine power of the Goddess within the human body. The transformative influence of this power leads to the activation of a person's latent centers of intuitive wisdom or Gnosis. They came to recognize this goddess power to be the alchemical "fire" that brought their experiments and rituals to completion.

From the Sufis, the Templars also learned that the eight pointed star, or cross, is both a symbol of the goddess as well as an ancient symbol for alchemy. The Templars, for this and other reasons, adopted it as their preeminent symbol. The Templars also venerated many other symbols of the goddess, such as the doves, roses, and five pointed stars. In fact, the controversial horned goat of Mendes, a symbol which the Templars made androgynous and adopted, which they also referred to as Baphomet, is actually a translation of Sophia the goddess.

From the Johannites, which emerged out of the Gnostic sect called the Essenes, the Templars were initiated into the Goddess rites and teachings brought to the Middle East from the Far East. It is this same Essene sect that Jesus was said to have been born into. Because of the influence of the Sufis, and the Johannites, the Templars came to know of the Holy Spirit as the power of the Goddess. It was this goddess power that the Knight's Templar attempted to transmit into their sacred ceremonies, and the same goddess power that they acknowledged to be the Holy Grail itself.

Statue of Pregnant Virgin Mary, Skępe, Poland

FIGURE 49

The Templars acquired knowledge of, and eventually passed along, highly guarded practices, such as the use of certain elixirs and herbs, which were consumed in an effort to catalyze alchemy inside themselves. The goal of these internal-alchemical processes was to awaken a latent force that exists at the base of the spine of all people. This force is known in the east as Kundalini, the 'serpent' power. Once this latent alchemical force is awakened within a person, it does all the work of purifying and transforming them until they acquire Gnosis. This force can also be awakened by a Gnostic master who has awakened and developed his or her own inner-kundalini.

Such transmissions are said to have occurred during initiation ceremonies of the Templars. At such times, Templar masters would transmit their own alchemical force into a new Templar, thereby initiating him onto the Gnostic path.

They learned tantric techniques that attempts to manipulate and/or transmute sexual energy, which in modern times is often associated with the genre called 'sex magick', a term coined by the late Freemason Aliester Crowley.

The Knights Templar and Freemasons are intimately related and, in fact, could be said to be in the same family. The Templars are the "big brothers" of the Masons, transmitting many of the secret traditions that were once part of the Templars into Freemasonry after the Templar order was dissolved in 1312.

Although Freemasonry, in its early form, existed long before the Templars formation in 1118, it was not so much a mystery tradition as it was an organization of operative masons that banded together and exchanged trade secrets. The form of modern Freemasonry that evolved after assimilating the Templar mysteries became known as Speculative Freemasonry, or "The Craft".

One example of a degree the Templars helped to create at this time was the degree of the Knight of the Rose Cross. The rights of this Masonic degree is said to be the same ones that the Templars themselves used among themselves.

Aleister Crowley (1875 - 1947)

FIGURE 50

Beginning in 1188, the Templars also brought into Europe wisdom gained from the Middle East. It is said that the three blue degrees come directly from the Sufi al'Banna. The Arabic word for Mason, is al'Banna, builder.

In 1307, after the inquisition, Templars who had fled to Scotland from France assisted in the transmission of their rites and secrets into what would eventually become the Scottish Rite of Freemasonry. The union of Freemasonry and Templarism was immortalized in stone in 1448 at Rosslyn Chapel.

The primary secrets that the Freemasons received were those related to alchemy; which is the process of transforming and evolving the human body. Through alchemy, a person is said to be able to tap into his or her innate store of gnostic or intuitive wisdom, and even achieve 'spiritual salvation'.

Today the alchemical influence of the Templars in Freemasonry can be found in the Masonic ideal of re-building Soloman's temple. This is a metaphor for re-building the human body through the alchemical power of Kabbalah.

The Kabbalistic significance of the 33 Degrees of Masonry, and other mystery schools, is easy to understand. There are 22 letters in the Hebrew alphabet divided into 3 groups:

> 3 Mother Letters
> 7 Double letters
> 12 Simple Letters.

There are 22 paths on the Kabbalistic Tree of Life and there are 11 Sephira (spheres / divine attributes) on the Tree. These are the 33 Degrees of Knowledge, and in Masonic lodges with 38 degrees, the other 5 degrees simply represent the 5 elements.

In astrotheology, the sun officially transitions into a new sign of the zodiac at the 33rd degree. In Michael Tsarion's book titled, "Astrotheology and Sidereal Mythology", he explains the occult association of "33" to the zodiac and the Sun this way:

Kabbalistic sage contemplates the Tree of Life

FIGURE 51

The sun enters at the 30th degree but is not totally clear until the 33rd degree, as it is of a certain size also. This is why they said in the Bible that the ministry of Christ begins at 30 and finishes at 33. This reference would have been unmistakable to anyone aware of the secrets of astrology. The number is connected to the initiation of the 'Sun' of god not 'Son,' passing through the zodiac. This is why the Freemasonic lodges also utilize the number.(34)

◇◇

The secret societies of Europe include Freemasonry, the Rosecrucians, and the Illuminati, some of which have vowed to get vengeance for the Knights Templars, who had been arrested and persecuted by the Inquisition and French monarchy.

The leadership of the Illuminati vowed not only to bring down the world's monarchies and fundamentalist religions, but it also resolved to dissolve any institution that imposed restriction on a person's freedom. This secret sect was formed to both follow the teachings of the Templars, as well as to create a one world spiritual tradition where gnostic and alchemical rites could be be universally shared and benefited from.

Everybody knows the traditional story of the founding of America. Christopher Columbus was an explorer who set sail in 1492 to enrich the Spanish monarchs with gold and spices from the orient. Not quite. During Columbus' lifetime, Jews became the target of persecution, culminating on March 31, 1492, when King Ferdinand and Queen Isabella proclaimed that all Jews were to be expelled from Spain. The edict especially targeted the 800,000 Jews who had never converted, and gave them just months to leave the territory.

The Jews who were forced to renounce Judaism and embrace Catholicism were known as "Conversos," or religious converts. There were also those who faked their conversion, practicing Catholicism outwardly while covertly practicing Judaism, the so-called "Marranos," which translates to pig or swine. Tens of thousands of Marranos were tortured by the Spanish Inquisition. They were pressured to offer names of friends and family members, who were ultimately paraded in front of crowds, tied to stakes and burned alive. Their land and personal possessions were then divvied up by the church and crown.

Recently, a number of Spanish scholars have concluded that Columbus was a Marrano, whose survival depended upon the suppression of all evidence of his Jewish background in face of the brutal, systematic ethnic cleansing. Columbus' voyage was not, as is commonly believed, funded by the deep pockets of Queen Isabella, but rather by two Jewish Conversos and another prominent Jew. Louis de Santangel and Gabriel Sanchez advanced an interest free loan of 17,000 ducats from their own pockets to help pay for the voyage, as did Don Isaac Abrabanel, rabbi and Jewish statesman. The first two letters Columbus sent back from his journey were not to Ferdinand and Isabella, but to Santangel and Sanchez, thanking them for their support and telling them what he had found. Columbus used a triangular signature of dots and letters that resembled inscriptions found on gravestones of Jewish cemeteries in Spain. He ordered his heirs to use the signature in perpetuity. According to British historian Cecil Roth's *The History of the Marranos*, the anagram was a cryptic substitute for the Kaddish, a prayer recited in the synagogue by mourners after the death of a close relative. Thus, Columbus' subterfuge allowed his sons to say Kaddish for their crypto-Jewish father when he died.

In Simon Weisenthal's book, "Sails of Hope," he argues that Columbus' voyage was motivated by a desire to find a safe haven for the Jews in light of their expulsion from Spain. Likewise, Carol Delaney, a cultural anthropologist at Stanford University, concludes that Columbus was a deeply religious man whose purpose was to sail to Asia to obtain gold in order to finance a crusade to take back Jerusalem and rebuild the Jews' holy Temple.

America, we were all taught in school, was named in honor of Amerigo Vespucci. It should be noted that his birth name was Alberigo Vespucci and his name change occurred after he return from the America's.

Author James Pyrse noticed that the chief god of the Mayan Indians in Central America was Quettzalcoatl. In Peru this god was called Amaru and the territory known as Amaruca. He writes that, "Amaruca is literally translated "Land of the Plumed Serpents." He then argues that the name of America was derived from Amaruca, instead of after the explorer Amerigo Vespucci. According to Manly P. Hall in *The Secret Teachings of All Ages*:

◇◇◇

These Children of the Sun adore the Plumèd Serpent, who is the messenger of the Sun. He was the God Quetzalcoatl in Mexico,

Gucumatz in Quiché; and in Peru he was called Amaru. From the latter name comes our word America. Amaruca is, literally translated, 'Land of the Plumèd Serpent.' The priests of this [flying dragon], from their chief center in the Cordilleras, once ruled both Americas. All the Red men who have remained true to the ancient religion are still under their sway. One of their strong centres was in Guatemala, and of their Order was the author of the book called Popol Vuh. In the Quiché tongue Gucumatz is the exact equivalent of Quetzalcoatl in the Nahuatl language; quetzal, the bird of Paradise; coatl, serpent—'the Serpent veiled in plumes of the paradise-bird'! (27)

◇◇◇

This origin of the name America is further reinforced by Jules Marcou, a prominent French geologist who studied in North America in the 19th-century, who reiterates that the name America was brought back to Europe from the New World and that Alberigo Vespucci had changed his name to reflect the name of this "new discovery".

Bibliography

1. Badlani , Hiro G. *Hinduism: Path of Ancient Wisdom*. iUniverse. (2008)

2. Johnson, W.J. *The Sauptikaparvan of the Mahabharata: The Massacre at Night*. Oxford University Press. (2008)

3. Sitchin, Zecharia. *The Case of the Evil Wind: Climate Study Corroborates Sumer's Nuclear Fate*. (2001)

4. The Bible. (Gen 18:27)

5. Datta, Amaresh. *The Encyclopaedia of Indian literature*. Volume two. Sahitya Akademi. (2006)

6. Sitchin, Zecharia. *The Wars of Gods and Men*. Harper. (1999)

7. Cullen, H.M. et al. "Climate change and the collapse of the Akkadian empire: Evidence from the deep sea". Geology. (April 2000)

8. deMenocal, Peter B. "Cultural Responses to Climate Change During the Late Holocenez". Journal Science. (April 2001)

9. Strutt, S.N. *Out of the Bottomless Pit*. Paragon publishing. (2014)

10. van Helsing, Jan, *Unternehmen Aldebaran*. Amadeus Verlag. (2003)

11. Jansen, Olaf. *A Voyage to the Inner World*. Chicago Forbes & Co. (1908)

12. "Horizon: Tutunkhamun's Fireball", made by production company TV6, was broadcast on BBC Two on Thursday, (July 20, 2006)

13. Pike, Albert. *Morals and Dogma of the Ancient and Accepted Scottish Rite of Freemasonry*. (1871)

14. Pauwels, Louis and Bergier, Jacques. *The Morning of the Magicians*. Stein and Day. (1960)

15. Gilbert, R. A. *The Supposed Rosy Crucian Society*. Peeters, (2001)

16. Lytton, Bulwer. *The Coming Race*. (1871)

17. Melanson, Terry. *The Vril Society, the Luminous Lodge and the Realization of the Great Work*. (2001)

18. Schwarzwaller, Wulf. *The Unknown Hitler: His Private Life and Fortune*. Natl Pr Books. (1988)

19. Steiger, Brad. *The Rainbow Conspiracy*. Kensington. (1998)

20. Kramers, Jan D., et al. "Unique chemistry of a diamond-bearing pebble from the Libyan Desert Glass strewnfield, SW Egypt: Evidence for a shocked comet fragment". Earth and Planetary Science Letters Volume 382, (November 2013)

21. *Science*. Vol. 311. no. 5765, p. 1223. (3 March 2006)

22. Longo, Giuseppe. *18: The Tunguska event*. Berlin Heidelberg New York (2007)

23. Dolan, Richard. "A Breakaway Civilization: What It Is, and What It Means for Us: Our Classified World." (April 2011)

24. Jonas, Hans. *New Testament studies: Society for New Testament Studies*. (1981)

25. Lennard, James. *Islam's Sacred Stone of Mecca*. (2009)

26. Tsarion, Michael. *Astrotheology and Sidereal Mythology*. Unslaved Media. (2012)

27. Hall, Manly P. *The Secret Teaching of all Ages*. (1928)

28. Meyer, Marvin, Robinson, James. *The Nag Hammadi Scriptures, International Edition*. HarperOne. (2007)

29. Lucian of Samosata. 200 AD. De Dea Syria

30. Wunderlich, H.G. *The Secret of Crete*. Souvenir Press Ltd., London. (1975)

31. Whitcombe, Cristopher. *Minoan Snake Goddess* (2000)

32. Condon, Christopher. *Did Hitler Escape to South America?* (2014)

33. Moore, Wes. *Hasan Bin Sabbah and the Secret Order of Hashishins.* (2001)

34. von Sebottendorff, Rudolf. *Secret Practices of the Sufi Freemasons: The Islamic Teachings at the Heart of Alchemy.* Inner Traditions, VT, (2013)

35. Newby, Gordon D. *A concise encyclopedia of Islam* (Repr. ed.). Oneworld. (2002)

36. Westcott, W. Wynn. *The Occult Power of Numbers.* p.15 (1911)

37. van Buren, Elizabeth. *The Secrets of the Illuminati.* (1983)

38. Zaehner, Robert Charles, *The Dawn and Twilight of Zoroastrianism,* New York: MacMillan, p. 163. (1961)

39. Herodotus, *Histories of Herodotus.* (c. 484 - 425 BCE); Translated by: George Rawlinson

40. Mair, Victor H., *Old Sinitic *Myag, Old Persian Magus and English Magician,* Early China 15: 27–47. (1990)

41. Icke, David. *The Biggest Secret.* (2000)

42. Frank, Joseph. *The Atlantis Encyclopedia.* (2008)

43. Westcott, William W. *Numbers: Their Occult Power and Mystic Virtues.* (1911)

44. The *Zend Avesta.* Part I, Vol. 4, translated by James Darmesteter (1880)

45. Wilson, Robert Anton and Robert Shea. *The Illuminatus! Trilogy.* (1975)

46. Moore, Wes. *Hasan Bin Sabbah and the Secret Order of Hashishins.* (2002)

47. Shatzmiller, Joseph. *Jews, Pilgrimage, and the Christian Cult of Saints: Benjamin of Tudela and His Contemporaries.* Toronto: University of Toronto Press.(1998)

48. Kohn, Livia. *Health and Long Life: The Chinese Way.* (2005)

49. Based on the Random House Dictionary, 2015.

50. Philo with an English Translation 1–10. Translated by F.H. Colson. Cambridge, Mass.: Harvard University Press. 1929–62.

51. Eason, Cassandra. *Fabulous Creatures, Mythical Monsters, and Animal Power Symbols: A Handbook.* Westport, CT, USA: Greenwood Publishing Group. p. 71 (2008)

52. Gimbutas, Marija. Robbins Dexter, Mirijam, ed. The living goddesses. Berkeley: University of California Press. pp. 157–158 (2001)

53. Deng, Y. "Ration of Qi with Modern Essential on Traditional Chinese Medicine Qi: Qi Set, Qi Element". Journal of Mathematical Medicine (2003)

54. Mullins, Eustace Clarence. *The World Order: Our Secret Rulers.* Ezra Pound Institute of Civilization. (1992)

55. Melanson, Terry. *The Vril Society, the Luminous Lodge and the Realization of the Great Work.* (2001)

56. Nichols, Preston., Moon, Peter. *Montauk Revisited: Adventures in Synchronicity.* Sky Books (1994)

Images

Figure 1 - Artistic depiction of a Vimana.

Figure 2 - Robert Oppenheimer and Albert Einstein. Alfred Eisenstaedt, Life Magazine. 1947.

Figure 3 - First atomic bomb dropped on the Bikini lagoon, on July 1, 1946.

figure 4 - Scan of Temple relief photo at Ellora caves, India.

Figure 5 - Tutankhamun's Pectoral with desert glass scarab, Egyptian Museum

Figure 6 - Scanned image of Lybian Desert Glass (LDG)

Figure 7 - Crater by test of first atomic bomb, Trinity in 1945

Figure 8 - Desert or Libyan Glass

figure 9 - Edward Bulwer-Lytton Portrait: A Portrait Gallery of Eminent Men and Women of Europe and America, with Biographies, by Evert A. Duykinck. New York: Johnson, Wilson and Company, 1873 (2 volumes).

Figure 10 - John Martin (1789–1854): Pandemonium, ca. 1825. Louvre Museum, Denon, 1st floor, room 32

Figure 11 - Alleged photograph of German craft, February 1945

Figure 12 - Scan of photo, Nazi flying wing

Figure 13 - Maria Orsic, Vril Society medium. Sketch by Angelica Manao-is (Angel Chewie Design)

Figure 14 - Robert Sepehr, Pergamon Museum, Berlin, Germany.

Figure 15 - Army of monkeys of Ramayana, Nakhon Ratchasima, Thailand

Figure 16 - Image first published in 1939 in *Atlantis: Mother of Empires* by Robert Stacy-Judd. Reprinted by David Hatcher Childress for *Adventures Unlimited* in 2007, with the following caption: "The picture was taken by Teobert Maler in a remote and at the time unknown spot deep in the jungles of Yucatan. Maler stated just prior to his death that the recorded scene was but a portion of a continuous frieze which surrounded the interior of an underground chamber."

Figure 17 - Trees knocked over by the Tunguska blast. Photo from the Soviet Academy of Science expedition led by Leonid Kulik

Figure 18 - Alleged Nazi sketch design of Haunabu craft

Figure 19 - Robert Sepehr, Pergamon Museum, Berlin, Germany.

Figure 20 - The archaeological remains of the Alamut Fortress as it stands today. Iran.

Figure 21 - Scanned photo of German U-boat

Figure 22 - Isabelita Peron, the third wife of Juan Peron and President of Argentina, this photo was July 1974 on the occasion of the funeral of Juan Peron.

Figure 23 - Photo display of the same Swastika symbol found in cultures of various nations.

Figure 24 - Adolf Hitler makes keynote address at Reichstag session, Kroll Opera House, Berlin, 1939

Figure 25 - Map of the Interior World in *The Goddess of Atvatabar,* by William Bradshaw, 1892

Figure 26 - An immaculately preserved 40,000 year old baby female woolly mammoth discovered on the banks of Siberia's Yuribei River in May 2007. Photo taken during a media preview in Hong Kong April 10, 2012.

Figure 27 - Hebrew prayer and Khamsa, a palm-shaped amulet

Figure 28 - Codices found at Nag Hammadi